SAND
in their
EYES

Thank you Linda

Chuck Doan as a baby in Vietnam

SAND
in their
EYES

one family's escape from post-war vietnam

CHUCK DOAN
with K. D. Winchester

Sand In Their Eyes

One Family's Escape from Post-War Vietnam

ISBN: 978-1-62020-524-2
eISBN: 978-1-62020-431-3

Cover Design & Page Layout by Hannah Nichols
eBook Conversion by Anna Riebe Raats

AE BOOKS
Emerald House
411 University Ridge, Suite B14
Greenville, SC 29601
www.ambassador-international.com

AMBASSADOR BOOKS
The Mount
2 Woodstock Link
Belfast, BT6 8DD, Northern Ireland, UK
www.ambassadormedia.co.uk

The colophon is a trademark of AE Books

ACKNOWLEDGEMENTS

I would like to thank my wife, Lisa, and our kids, Kenny and Kayle, for all of their support as I have pursued writing this book. I would also like to thank, Mom Nguyễn Thị Của, Dad Đoạn Van Đạt, my brothers—Trường, Phong, and An—and my sisters—Loan and Amy Diem. Many thanks to my uncles, aunts, and all my cousins. I am also very grateful for Lisa's parents, Nguyễn Huu Quyen and Nguyễn Thi Gioi for their support over the years.

Thank you to our sponsors to America—Kent and Donna Garlinghouse, Cynthia and C.J. White, Jan Bergherr, David Weiss, and the Kelseys: Michael, Pamela, Margot and Maxwell—for helping make my story possible. I would also like to thank Miss Beverly and Mr. John, the librarian and the teacher who helped me at the refugee camp in the Philippines. Also thanks to Mom Suzanne and Dad Jeff Granger for taking me in and treating me like their own son. Their kindness forever changed my life.

Thanks to two of our sponsors, Bob Saxon and Jon Rogers for the photos, for providing us with pictures from the war, and much appreciation to our clients and friends from J Nails, LLC. And a very special thank you to Sarah Stephenson for pushing me to tell my story. Without her help to begin this project, this book wouldn't have been possible.

Thanks to Sam and Tim Lowry at Ambassador for making my dream possible, and thank you Sara, Hannah, and Anna for working hard to put the book together and make it look so great.

Of course, so much thanks to Kendra Winchester who helped give voice to my story and make this book possible. You have captured not only my family's story, but also our emotions and feelings. Thank you for your patience and for sharing this journey with me.

An addition, I thank Claire Petersen, Autumn Privett, Elizabeth Turner, Samuel Winchester, and Stephanie Wright for working as peer readers and editors.

To all the Vietnam veterans, I cannot thank you enough for everything that you have done for me and for my family. Ultimately, this book is for you.

Sponsors and Supporters

Jon Rogers

Second Lieutenant

25th Infantry Division

Bob Saxon

175th Assault Helicopter Company Outlaw CW2

Dr. Jay and Mrs. Kim Walls

Lisa and Brian Watson, LTC

Mark and Lisa Yost

INTRODUCTION

THIS BOOK HAS BEEN A long time coming. Dreams do come true, and for those of you whose dreams haven't come true yet, don't give up. Just keep going, and they will come true for you. I know that's a fact for me.

I would like to thank all of you from the bottom of my heart for reading my book. I have wanted to write this book for years now, to share my story. I loved the American soldiers that I met as a boy. These men were always kind and generous to me, and I have never forgotten them. I equally admired the GIs and South Vietnamese soldiers who bravely fought alongside one another and died for my country's freedom.

I would like to take this opportunity to thank the GIs who sacrificed so much in the Vietnam War for a country and a people that they did not even know. I know now, since I have come to live here, that's what Americans do. Though not everyone agrees about the Vietnam War, I will never forget how American soldiers helped defend South Vietnamese liberty and freedom.

Since I have come to America, the continuing misconception about the war has broken my heart. I lived under communism for nine years. The Vietcong came, and our lives changed. Many South Vietnamese people fled with the GIs instead of staying to face the Vietcong. Later, families like mine left, despite the small chance of survival, rather than staying in Vietnam. We left our culture, our home, our country, and our families to escape the horrors that the Vietcong brought. I will always appreciate how the Americans sacrificed so much for my people, tried to liberate us from the Vietcong, and welcomed us into their country.

Many people take liberty and freedom for granted. I would like to say that the South Vietnamese people, our military and our families, are still appreciative for all the GIs that died and sacrificed for the South Vietnamese people. I want the GIs' families to know that their loved ones—their sons, their daughters, their husbands, their wives—did not die in vain. They died and sacrificed for a great cause—for liberty and freedom for the South Vietnamese people. I hope that reading my book gives some people closure. Through my story, I want people to know that there is hope and that there is always light at the end of the tunnel. If I learned anything from my ordeals, it is that you cannot change the past, but you can always choose to move forward.

Thank you,

Chuck Doan

LIST OF FAMILY MEMBERS

FATHER'S SIDE

Ống Nội (Đoạn Hữu Thành) - Paternal Grandfather

Bà Nội - (Nguyễn Thi Triệu) Paternal Grandmother

Chủ Sâu (Đoạn van Phục) - Oldest Uncle

Chủ Bảy (Đoạn Văn Ảnh) - Middle Uncle

Thiem Bảy (Nguyễn Thị Gương) - Chủ Bảy's Wife

Chủ Út (Đoạn Trúng Hưởng) - Youngest Uncle

MOTHER'S SIDE

Bà Ngoại (Vợ Thi Sau) - Maternal Grandmother

Cầu Tam (Nguyễn Van Gam) -Younger Uncle

Cầu Út (Nguyễn Van Son)- Youngest Uncle

Đường Bảy (Nguyễn Thôn) - Mother's Brother-in-law

Nguyễn Thị Bến - Đường Bảy's Daughter

IMMEDIATE FAMILY

Ba (Đoạn Van Đạt) - Father

Má (Nguyễn Thị Của)- Mother

Tuần (Chuck) - Me
Trường (Đoạn Nhát Truống) - Brother
Phong (Đoạn Tuấn Phong) - Younger Brother
Loan (Đoạn Phường Loan) - Sister
An (Đoạn Trường An) - Youngest Brother

OTHERS

Bác Hai (Nguyễn Văn Hài) - Former Military Captain
Nguyễn Bé Tủ - Bác Hai's Son

PROLOGUE

TWO AMERICAN SOLDIERS RAN TOWARDS the helicopter. In front of them, more GIs beckoned urgently from the waiting chopper. Behind them was absolute chaos. Soldiers ran around yelling conflicting orders, frantically doing something, anything to prepare for the inevitable. A few stood by watching stoically. The smells of smoke and gasoline filled the air. Piles of paper, anything that could be incriminating, were burning.

As the GIs reached the waiting helicopter, hands reached down to help them in. Then the chopper lifted off, the loud whir of blades barely drowning out the sound of the frightened Vietnamese below. The Americans crowded into the aircraft, watched the scene below them, and looked at each other, relief clearly visible on their young, strained faces.

This was Vietnam in April 1975. The final days of American involvement in the Vietnam War were consumed with the urgent effort to evacuate all American personnel. North Vietnamese artillery pounded Saigon, and tanks began pushing into the city. The soldiers left behind a nation entirely destroyed by war.

By some measures, the evacuation was a success. The American soldiers escaped further harm and managed to take nearly 140,000 refugees with them on large transport ships. But those left behind—soldiers of the South Vietnamese army, government officials and their entire families—were now targets. They had resisted the Communists, and that was not an offense quickly forgiven.

At long last, the bloody war was over, but the battle to survive was just beginning.

The 175th assault helicopter co. about to enter Takeo Cambodia in 1970

CHAPTER ONE

MY LAST TWO MARBLES SEEMED to sweat as I rolled them around and around my palm. All of us boys stood in a face-off in Hung's bare front yard with just a dirt circle between the two opposing sides. As the heat shimmered from the rippling sides of the aluminum houses, we all gathered around as if preparing for a fight. And I was the first one up.

The boy across the dirt circle in front of me smirked a little as he set up his handful of flashing glass. I had to win this time, or I would have nothing left. We played for keeps. So I took a deep breath, set up my marbles, and prepared for battle.

"Just focus, Tuần. You can beat him; he can't hit a marble to save his life," said Tam.

Glancing over at him, I pulled back my two front fingers to stretch them out. "He's good," I said.

"But you're better," said Tam. How I would have loved to believe him.

Someone called for the start . . . the countdown . . . and go! I pulled back my fingers and flicked my marble towards the marble in the center. The center marble needed to be knocked into the hole on the other side— before my opponent knocked his center marble into the hole on my side. Marbles clicked across the circle, barely heard over cheering boys.

"Come on, Tuần! Hit his marble! Knock it out!" My fingers felt on fire and it became harder to send my marble in the right direction. Close.

13

So close. I saw my opponent flick his fingers with one last thwack as I struggled to knock my marble into the hole.

Cheers erupted around me. My heart sank as my face flushed in shame. But suddenly I felt a hand beating my back and heard Tam yelling in my face, "You won! You won,Tuần!"

Boys dropped sticky marbles that I had won into my palms. I was dazed, hardly believing what had just happened. But my victory was short lived as I was shoved aside while the two new boys prepared to play. Stunned, I stood outside the huddle of boys and stared into space. The road in front of the house led down to the market. The road was eerily quiet, and the heat still pressed down on us. Just another day in South Vietnam.

The sound of shouting boys drew me back into the game, and I shoved my new marbles into my pockets, leaning over the circle.

But a high, motherly voice interrupted the game, calling, "Tam! Tam, come home! Come home now!"

Tam's eyes lowered in embarrassment as other boys snickered and teased him, "Come home, Tam. Come home, little boy."

Annoyed, Tam shoved boys aside and began to stand, but he fell back, as if a massive hand forced him down. I felt the sound before I heard it. A wave of pressure filled my ears, followed by the blast of an explosion. At the same moment the ground beneath us moved, marbles scattered, and boys flew and rolled on top of one another.

Seconds, minutes—time was immeasurable. Tremor after tremor rolled beneath us. Then I heard the screams.

Bruised but okay, my friends and I staggered to our feet and began to run. We ran toward the market, toward the screams. The road had been blown into a shallow crater by the bomb, and debris and ash still floated down from the sky. The people in the market—the man that sold my morning

A market similar to the one destroyed

sticky bun, the woman that made the best pot-stickers—had suddenly been obliterated. Instead of the familiar noises of price haggling and vendors shouting their wares, the sound of war filled my ears. People shouted for loved ones. A man lifted a woman into his arms, calling her name, begging for her to respond. He didn't even seem to notice that half her face was gone.

For the second time that day, my heart plunged into my chest, but this time it stayed there, gnawing its way deeper inside until I felt nothing but horror. Nothing I had felt before truly compared to this moment. I began to back away, but my foot hit something—something that was not just debris on the road. I looked down to see an arm lying on the ground, still covered in scraps of a sleeve.

Since the bombing had been moving closer to Cần Thơ, the city where we lived, my father had made sure that we had a bunker in our house. He had dug out a shallow hole underneath my grandparents' bed, creating a wall around the hole with cinderblock. He had put a slab of cement on top of the cinderblocks to create a small shelter. After it was finished, my father told me that if anything ever happened, if we were ever bombed or attacked, I was to go there.

Back across the ditch and down the sidewalk I ran, through my front gate, into the house and underneath the bed. I wriggled down into the dark, curling into a ball. I tried to slow my breathing, as if, somehow, becoming as silent as possible would keep me safe from the screams out-side. But the air was stifling, and the cement dust filled my nose and lungs, making calming my mind impossible.

Shutting my eyes made no difference; I still saw the horrors of the marketplace, the mutilation of people who had been alive just a few min-utes ago. I couldn't forget the faces of those screaming for the ones they had just lost.

I waited for what seemed like hours, but I am sure it must have been only a few minutes. The hum of silence finally broke when someone called my name, "Tuấn, are you here?"

I scurried from my hiding place. Relief filled me almost as fast as the fresh air entering my lungs. There was my mother, safe and sound. She grabbed me, checking me all over for cuts or bruises. "I am fine. I am fine, Má." We were all fine, but many of our neighbors weren't.

That day was the first day that I saw the war with my own eyes.

———————————

Before the bombing of the marketplace, I hadn't noticed how hor-rible the war could be. During the Vietnam War when the Americans were here, life was good. When my father joined the South Vietnamese military and began working for the Americans as combat engineer, my parents moved my two younger brothers and me to Cần Thơ. We had a nice middle-class house in the suburbs, and my grandparents lived in the house next door. Because of the war, food may not have been in abun-dance, but we didn't starve.

We felt the most stress when my father had to leave for trips out closer to the front, returning every three or four weeks. While he was away, my mother and grandmother worried constantly. But he always came home, and I remember that he would bring back American rations, which seemed like a special treat to me.

Two of my father's brothers also joined the South Vietnamese military and helped the Americans; Chủ Sáu worked as a translator in an American military office, and Chủ Bảy was a South Vietnamese marine. Chủ Sáu, in particular, made friends with the American soldiers, often bringing them back to our house. I adored their visits. The GIs always brought candy and strange American trinkets for my brothers and me. One time they came and I ran up to them, screaming with joy and shoving my hand in the side pocket of one of the GI's cargo pants. Something bit me. I screamed, this time in fright, and snatched my hand back. The soldier laughed and pulled out a plastic lizard he had put there for just such an occasion. To this day I remember how they played with my brothers and me, these white strangers fighting for our freedom. Despite the dangers they faced every day, they still had time for us.

After that bombing, it all changed. Looking back on it, I am sure things had been changing in South Vietnam for a while. Ba would later talk about the Paris Peace Accords of 1973, when the president of the U.S. signed a treaty agreeing to withdraw American soldiers from Vietnam in exchange for American prisoners of war. But as a five-year-old in early 1974, I had been oblivious. One time before the marketplace bombing, when Ba was away, the entire family was eating dinner, and a large explosion sounded in the distance, shaking our house and sending dishes smashing to the ground. My family headed for the bunker underneath my grandparents' bed, but three adults and three children could barely fit into the small space. The experience left an impression of stuffy air that smelled like cement and human bodies. Despite the initial terror, I hadn't seen the damage from the explosion—people killed, families torn apart. It had just been some smashed pots. Pots could be replaced.

———————

So that evening when I sat in front of our little house and watched the soldiers and citizens alike running back and forth to the marketplace and the helicopters flying overhead, I realized that this war was for real—it was drawing closer.

My grandfather, Ông Nội, came outside and sat with me. My grandparents, my father's parents, had the house that was connected to ours by the kitchen on the back porch. As the oldest grandson of their oldest son, I was the favorite. Like most Asian cultures, the Vietnamese prize their heritage and hold family honor as one of the great, if not the greatest, traditions to uphold. Since my father was usually on assignment out in the field, Ông Nói made sure to take me to school every morning and always bought me breakfast from one street vendor or another. We would chat about school, and he would warn me to stay out of trouble, which of course I never did.

"You gave us a scare today, Tuần," said Ông Nội. "We didn't see you when you ran home from the explosion." I felt too horrible to respond. I had been so scared.

Ông Nội must have seen the look on my face because he quickly reassured me. "I am not angry. You saw something horrible today, and you got to the bunker like we told you," he said. "But I guess we knew you could run fast." He laughed and swatted my leg which had a healing cut up its side.

I smiled, knowing he was trying to make me feel better by reminding me of the time my friends and I had been picking on a girl in our class.

She was always a bit slow, so of course as kids we felt that gave us every right to tease her. When I yelled my insult at her, her face turned red, filling with anger. I suddenly knew I had gone too far. I ran. I ran all the way back to my own house with the girl screaming insults right behind me. I never knew how she ran as fast as she did, keeping pace with me block after block. When I finally reached my house, the front gate was locked, meaning that a fence of barbed wire stood between me and my front door. But the girl was right behind me, so when no one answered my screams to open the gate, I jumped the fence, slicing my leg. But as I tracked blood to the back of the house, I didn't care. It had been Ông Nội that had to patch up my leg and try not to laugh as he told me that I better not pick on that girl again because she would "most certainly kick my butt" if she got ahold of me. It seemed Ông Nội was always the one bailing me out of the trouble I found.

"You will have to tell your father of your adventures when he comes home," said Ông Nội.

I tried to smile, but I couldn't helping thinking, *but what if he doesn't come home this time?*

When my mother, my siblings, and I stayed home, tucked away safe from the major violence from the war—for the most part—we never saw a lot of violence, but we heard of it. The artillery sounded in the distance more and more as the Vietcong drew closer. Even now, years after the war, the sound of helicopters over my head or artillery on the news takes me back to Vietnam, as if the sounds have created in me a permanent response.

As the war progressed, my father's assignments away from us grew longer and longer, with shorter visits home. We never knew when he would turn up, or for how long he would be able to stay. We just had to learn to enjoy the time we had.

"He will come, Tuấn. He will come," said Ông Nội. Ông Nội always seemed to have hope.

My eyes roamed down the street that was mostly empty now, and I thought of my two younger brothers and my mother. I had to take better care of them now. I remembered right before Ba left for the war, he sat down with me, explaining that he would be gone more and didn't know how much he could be home. I said, "I am a big boy now. I will take care of Má and my brothers." My father hugged me tightly, and then he was gone. I had to be the man now.

━━━━━━━

Ông Nội made his way down to the head of the table, slowly lowering himself down to sit on the floor. I sat on the other end near my younger brother, Trường, who was telling my mother that he was not too young to eat the crunchy rice in the bowl this time. At the bottom of every rice pot, some rice burnt and grew crunchy. Everyone wanted a bit of this rice, like it was a dessert, and my grandparents would always tease that we wouldn't get any this time. We were just too young. Later when I ate ice cream or drank soda in front of my kids, I'd say, "You're not old enough," just like Ông Nội.

"Ma, I am four. I am not a baby like Phong." Bà Nội, my grandmother, held my youngest brother, Phong, who wiggled and chattered at hearing his name.

Má was just bringing out the pot of rice and setting it beside the bowl of soup already on the table.

"Soft rice for young teeth. That is the best way," teased Ông Nội.

"But I am not—" began Trường.

"You will get some," Má interrupted. "You need to be silent and eat your food. Now sit." When Má talked liked this, we knew not to argue, and I wondered if it was because I had scared her that day. But maybe it was something else. Má didn't look at any of us, but took our bowls and filled them one by one.

Like she did every night, Má gave food first to Ông Nội and Bà Nội, then me and Trường. As long as I could remember, my parents had explained that we must show respect to our elders, which is why Ông Nội and Bà Nội always received their food first; they deserved the greatest honor. The rest of our family was like that too. Each family member needed to respect their elders—even younger to older siblings.

This is why Ông Nội always got the fish head, what we considered to be the best part. I watched as Ông Nội pulled his bowl towards himself, steaming fish head sitting on top of his pile of rice. *One day, I will get the fish head*, I thought. When I was older and head of the family, I could have all the fish head and crunchy rice I wanted. I peered into my own bowl filled with rice and pieces of fish. The scent of fish and garlic wafted into my nose, and my body suddenly realized it hadn't eaten in several hours—not since before the bombing.

I picked up my bowl and lifted it close to my mouth, using my chopsticks to shovel food as quickly as possible. The faster I ate, the more likely I would be able to get more. "Slow down before you choke yourself," said Má.

Since we didn't have a way to store leftover food, my mother cooked only what we could eat. But I saw that after everyone had received their food, there was a small portion left. I guessed I would be eating those leftovers for breakfast tomorrow. Suddenly we heard something from inside the house. Má's head lifted in an instant, eyes pressing against the door to see where the noise came from. *It's not exploding stuff or anything else scary like before. So what is it?* I thought. In a few moments, my father stepped through the door into the main room.

My mother cried out and ran to him.

Soon, Ba was swarmed and brought to the table where he sat down. Má piled all the food we had left into his bowl. I knew I wouldn't eat the leftovers for breakfast tomorrow morning.

"Come, tell us what is going on out beyond Cần Thơ. What is going on in the war?" asked Ông Nội.

"Ông Nội, let him eat!" said Bà Nội. "He looks as thin as a toothpick. He needs his strength."

"Yes, you're right," said Ông Nội, but he didn't seem to be able to sit still as my father finished every last grain of rice.

My mother began clearing the pots and bowls off the table, and my grandmother started moving the little kids to bed. They moved quickly in and out, preparing tea and cleaning, but I am sure that they could hear every word. I was older than my brothers, so as long as I was quiet, I could stay.

"So how are your brothers? Have you heard from them?" asked Ông Nội. Bà Nội stopped whatever she was doing to listen.

My father paused before he spoke, "I have not heard from them this time, Ba. But a friend of mine says that he has heard that they are still alive, but I don't know anything beyond that."

The room seemed to let out its breath with my grandfather's smile. "Thank heavens that they are safe. And you, my son, how are you? What is it like out there?" said Ông Nội.

My father looked at me but did not send me away; instead, he just looked at the table a moment before pulling out a cigarette. Ông Nội hated

Ba's cigarettes, but Ba had heard his arguments before, so Ông Nội didn't saying anything. Before Ba could answer Ông Nội's questions, Má and Bà Nội came in with the tea. Both women served my father and grandfather tea from porcelain cups before sitting down on the bed across from the table.

As my father began to explain his job, or as much of it as he would while I was in earshot, I went and sat on the bed near Bà Nội and laid my head down in her lap. As the adults talked, they seemed to forget that I was there.

"So the Vietcong are getting closer," said Ông Nói.

Ba nodded and said, "It won't be long now. The Americans withdraw a little more everyday. The South Vietnamese army are having to help themselves with the Americans' support. If only they would just give us their guns and ammunition when they leave. We don't have the resources to keep fighting."

Ba continued to describe how the South Vietnamese president came to America and asked not for help, but for ammunition. The South Vietnamese military was *that* short on resources. Ông Nội paused and seemed to want to say something. At first I thought he was saying something that I couldn't hear, so I listened as hard as I could. I needed to know what was going on.

"Then I think it's time to prepare to move out to the village," said Ông Nội.

"So you wish to die?" said Bà Nói. She spoke so suddenly that I jumped, reminding her of my presence. I felt her hand on my head and shut my eyes. Hopefully they would keep talking.

"Don't speak like that. You'll bring us bad luck," said Ông Nội. I opened my eyes, afraid that my grandmother had made Ông Nội very angry, but he didn't seem upset. His eyes seemed more worried than anything else, but also determined. "At the farm in the village, we can leave before the Vietcong come and take everything away from us. Who knows what will happen if we stay here?"

"And if we leave now, we will be killed even before the Vietcong arrive!" said Bà Nói.

"Ba, Má is right. We shouldn't go out so soon. Just wait a little, and we'll see what happens. I'll see what I can find out when I leave tomorrow," said my father.

"Tomorrow?" said my mother. I thought the same thing. *Hadn't he just come home? Didn't he need time to rest before he went away again?*

"Yes," said Ba, "I managed to come home to see you tonight, but I leave in the morning."

I looked at Má sitting beside Bà Nói. Má looked into her lap, and I knew she was trying not to show that she was upset. She began to raise her head, and I shut my eyes tight so she couldn't see me watching her.

Soon after that, Bà Nói put me to bed. Ba came in a while later to see if I was awake.

"Tuần," he said.

"Yes?"

"You know I have to leave tomorrow." He paused. "You need to take care of your mother now. When I am gone, you need to be the man of the house."

I nodded and hugged him before lying back down and drifting off to sleep. I was determined to wake up in time to say goodbye to Ba, but when I woke up the next morning, he was already gone. I worried that he would be okay. I didn't know where exactly he went on these trips, but if the Vietcong were getting closer, were they closer to us or to Ba?

CHAPTER TWO

ÔNG NỘI TOLD ME STORIES, mythology, from Vietnam's history. My favorite stories were about Kim Quy, the Golden Turtle who helped Vietnamese heroes throw off the shackles of rulers who had occupied Vietnam.

Ông Nội told me that much of the first 15 centuries AD were consumed with the battle for who would dominate the region. One time around AD 200, Kim Quy helped an emperor throw off the ruling family by gifting the man with a crossbow. Another time, a peasant named Lê Lợi led a revolution against the Chinese with a magical sword named "Heaven's Will." Some people say that Kim Quy gave him the sword, but others insist that Lê Lợi found it by chance. Lê Lợi overthrew the Chinese and became emperor, beginning the Lê Dynasty. One day, Lê Lợi visited a beautiful lake—and was shocked to see Kim Quy rising out of the water. Kim Quy asked for the sword back, and Lê Lợi threw it into the lake. Kim Quy grabbed the sword in his mouth and disappeared beneath the surface, and the sword was never seen again. The Lê Dynasty did not fall until 350 years later, and ever since, no single ruler of Vietnam has been able to hold on for very long.

During my childhood, every child in South Vietnam learned that the Portuguese had come to Vietnam around the 17th century, built a port, and established a trading center. To gain the advantage over his rivals, Emperor Gia Long requested French assistance, which was readily provided because the French had striven unsuccessfully for decades to gain a piece of the valuable trade in that region. Once invited, though, the French proved troublesome allies. The Catholic missionaries the French brought with them were unwelcome, and the emperor, Anh, and his successors began purging the nation of the missionaries and their converts.

By 1840, French Catholics called for military intervention to stop the slaughter, but it wasn't until 1857 that Napoleon III finally sent troops to Vietnam. By then, control of trade was once again the main concern. For the next forty years, France would violently assert its influence in the region until it finally established the Indochinese Union, consisting mainly of modern-day Vietnam, Cambodia, and Laos.

French rule from the 1860s onward was not peaceful. Many improvements were made to the region, and some promising intellectuals were invited to study in France, but the majority of the region labored under the heavy-handed political and religious rule of the French. Vietnamese people were forced to convert to Catholicism. If they refused, they endured torture and risked their families being threatened, or worse, killed. For one hundred years, Vietnam simmered, growing ever closer to an explosion that seemed all too inevitable.

By the time the Vietcong began to take control of Vietnam, our country was ready for real change. Tired of outside powers taking control of our country, the people of Vietnam seemed all too ready to once again throw off the shackles of a ruling power. Starting in the north, the Vietcong slowly moved south, charming the Vietnamese where the French abuse had been the worst. However, as the Vietcong moved south, the Southern Vietnamese were more hesitant to join the communist cause. By the time the Vietcong reached the countryside where our family lived in a village outside of Cần Thơ, the Vietcong was proclaiming that the Americans, who had begun to step in to stop the growing spread of communism, were just like the French who had terrorized the Vietnamese. "We must all be good citizens and join communism, a government run by our own people," they said. But Ông Nội wasn't convinced. For every person charmed by the Vietcong, another one spread whispers of the Vietcong's true nature—violent and cruel.

The Vietcong began harassing my grandfather's village, and Ba and his brothers thought that if they joined the communists, they would be safe from the Vietcong and leave the family alone. When Ông Nội learned that his sons were planning to join the communists, he went to where he knew the communists were hiding out and demanded that his sons come home. If they didn't, my grandfather said he would kill himself. Though they desired freedom and respect for the Vietnamese people, respect and love for my grandfather meant more to them than any cause or promise. So they followed him home.

To avoid any further contact with the communists, Ông Nội moved the family to Cần Thơ, to the safety of numbers and distance. After years of French rule, Ông Nội knew all too well how unprotected the country villagers were to outside invaders. He wanted to give us all a chance at a better life.

Now it was 1974 and I was five-years-old. Ông Nội knew another decision must be made—to stay in Cần Thơ or to leave. If the Vietcong won the war, our family would have to flee the city immediately. After he considered my father's and Bà Nội's advice, Ông Nội decided to move us to the farm. The weekend after my father's brief visit, my grandfather went out to the farm to start cleaning up the property. While we had been in the city, our farm out in the village hadn't been in use. It needed some repairs, and the land needed to be cleared for planting.

Over the next few years, our family wondered if things would have been different if Ông Nội had made a different decision. Bà Nội discarded such speculation, always saying that what was meant to be will be.

Ông Nội took my youngest uncle, Chủ Út, with him to the farm for the weekend. That first day, they worked all morning, cutting down the tall grass in the fields. The heat was terrible, the air thick with humidity, but Ông Nội was determined to get as much done during their trip as possible. Around midday, Chủ Út suggested they eat. Reluctantly, Ông Nội agreed. But wanting to complete as much of the field as possible, Ông Nội told Chủ Út, "Just go start getting the food together, and I will meet you over at the house."

My uncle agreed and started towards the house, squelching through the mud and cut grass. But then he heard a *click*. He froze. Was he on a mine?

An explosion ripped towards him from behind, throwing my uncle off of his feet. Chủ Út hadn't stepped on a mine; Ông Nội had. Chủ Út staggered to his feet, turned, and ran to Ông Nội, who was lying face down in the grass. Rolling Ông Nội onto his back, my uncle saw that my grandfather's face was pitted with shrapnel. The village had no hospital, not even a clinic, so my uncle had to carry Ông Nội to their little boat, about the size of a canoe, and row him down the river to the nearest hospital in the city.

By the time Chủ Út reached the hospital, my grandfather was dead, and Uncle was torn with grief. If only he had watched the ground more carefully for mines. If only he had made Ông Nội go back with him for lunch. If only he had rowed a little faster. But there was nothing he could have done. We later found out that the mine wasn't even from the Vietcong; it was one of ours, one from the South Vietnamese.

Chủ Út left the hospital to go home to tell Bà Nội and Má. When he came in the door, Bà Nội immediately knew something was wrong. Where was Ông Nội? Why wasn't he with him? Chủ Út told her. Bà Nội screamed and fell to the ground, wailing, "No, no, no!"

Má and I heard the scream and came running over, fearing the worst. I had never heard such a sound before, and it wouldn't be the last time.

I saw Bà Nội on the ground, Chủ Út crying as he said something to Má. She started to cry too, and I didn't understand. I screamed for someone to let me know what was happening, so my mother kneeled down and told me, her face puffy with tears, that my Ông Nội, my grandfather, was dead.

"No, I don't believe it," I said. "No, Ông Nội's not dead!" I screamed, shouting that I didn't believe it, over and over.

My uncle grabbed me, forcing me to be still and shushing me. "Ông Nội's at the hospital, Tuấn. Shhh. . . . We will go see him tomorrow." After a while of listening to my uncle's reassurances, I calmed down, sniffling as a numbness crept over me. Ông Nội? Dead? No, he was at the hospital, so he must be just sick, right? I would see him tomorrow.

But Bà Nội and Má left immediately for the hospital and did not come home that night. When my uncle, my brothers, and I reached the hospital, I knew for sure that Ông Nội was not sick. He really was dead.

I didn't know at the time that my uncle had already told our neighbors to give the word to my father's oldest sister—it was time to call in the family. My father and uncles in the military all received leave to come home and bury Ông Nội. In Vietnamese culture, it is respectful to bury a man on the same land where he is born. For my grandfather, this meant taking him back out to the village, right near where the Vietcong had been sighted. My father's aunt, Ông Nội's sister, argued that it was too dangerous to take my grandfather's body out that far. "No more death," she said. "Please, no more death."

But my father, now head of the family, insisted that they pay the greatest honor and respect to Ông Nội. They would take him back to the country to be buried.

A Vietnamese funeral prepares the deceased loved one's spirit for the afterlife. The monk led us in prayer every hour, and every hour we performed the ritual with bowing prayer and burning incense that filled the air with smoke to please Ông Nội's spirit. All of the family wore differing degrees of traditional white funeral clothes, from my father's full set of robes and head dress to the smallest little boy's plain white headband. Each family member's level of mourning reflected their place in the family.

After a day of prayer, the family prepared for the funeral procession to Ông Nội's burial place. I remember looking at the plain, wooden casket, and I just couldn't bear the thought of saying goodbye. He couldn't leave me like this—I had to see him. I told my father that I wanted to see Ông Nội, but my father didn't want me to see Ông Nội broken and bruised, torn apart from the shrapnel. Though my father kept insisting that I shouldn't see him, I screamed, demanded, to see Ông Nội. Finally, my father relented, holding me up to the open casket. I sobbed even harder, but I said goodbye.

Later as I walked in front of the procession of the casket to the burial place, I just kept thinking what this would mean. Who would walk me to school? Help me with my homework? Was I the man of the house now? We all gathered around the graveside, and the monk prayed over the casket as we laid my grandfather to rest.

From the place he came, so should he be buried.

My father and two uncles had to return to the field shortly after the funeral service, giving them only a few days to handle my grandfather's affairs. Before he left, my father saw me crying and told me, "Tuấn, men don't cry. Real men shed blood, not tears."

I was shocked. Ông Nội was gone. How could I stop this sadness from overflowing out of my heart? Didn't Ba feel anything? At first I was angry at what Ba had said, but Má took me in her arms, whispering, "Ignore him, Tuấn. Your father is just trying to be tough, but on the inside he is just as sad as you are."

"But he said that; he said *that*. He doesn't understand!" I cried.

After Ba and my uncles left, we couldn't ignore the silent emptiness that pressed in on our lives. My Bà Nội and Má sewed blackened patches of cloth on our clothes, and I would often walk into Bà Nội's house to find her praying to Buddha and burning incense for Ông Nội's spirit.

One of the first nights after Ba and my uncles left, I began to set the table, pulling out only the few bowls and sets of chopsticks that we would need. When Má came in with the food, she paused and said, "Tuấn, where is your grandfather's place? Why didn't you get his bowl and chopsticks."

I paused, confused. Didn't she remember that Ông Nội was dead?

Má looked at me for a moment, and her face relaxed. Setting down the food, she said, "Come here, Tuấn." She knelt down and faced me. "I know Ông Nội has passed, but we must honor his spirit and set a place for him like we always have. Not forever. But for a while."

And we did. All throughout the next year, the last year of the war, we set a place at the table for Ông Nội until the first anniversary of his death. After that, we set a place for him every anniversary of his passing to remember and honor the man whom we had loved and lost.

Though it may have been hard for me to imagine, life continued after Ông Nội's death in a fairly normal way. But it was Bà Nội who now walked me to school. Sometimes we would stop by the food stalls, but the food tasted bitter to me without Ông Nội, until soon it hurt too much to stop by at all.

Bà Nội was distracted; she constantly worried about my father and uncles who were out in the jungle fighting the Vietcong. Death had become an ever-present reality as every day more rumors of the Vietcong filtered into the city. "They are coming," someone would whisper around a food stall. "They are almost here," a neighbor would whisper. We didn't know who to believe.

Several months after Ông Nội's funeral, more bombs and artillery began going off in the city. With my father and uncles gone, Má and Bà Nội had to find a way to take care of my brothers and me. We spent days in the tiny bomb shelter, trying to breathe in the hot, suffocating air. We would run out of food and water, but we still had to wait. At first there were bombings only a few times a month, but by the end of war there seemed to be nothing but explosions. In the rare silences, Má or Bà Nội would run out to cook us whatever food they had or run to the market to buy more food.

I remember how much the house shook, my brothers crying with fear. The air seemed permanently thick with debris; I couldn't breathe. Even today, as I watch the news coverage of the war in the Middle East, I see the explosions and military choppers on the television screen, and I remember. I understand.

In April 1975, the war was coming to a close, and we were losing. At the time I knew that losing was a bad thing, but then the war would be over, my father would finally be home, and the bombing would stop. Even if I had known, I would never have completely understood that all I had ever known—our house, our family, our way of life—would never be the same.

While my family had been huddled in our little bunker, my father had been out in the field. That last year of the war, I could count on one hand how many times Ba had been home. But I still waited for him, never losing hope that today might be the day he came home. One day I asked my mother why he had to be gone so much. She said, "Your Ba is helping to fight the Vietcong to keep us safe."

But I persisted, "Why are the Vietcong fighting us? Why don't they just leave us alone?"

For once my mother didn't sidestep my questions. Instead she explained that the Vietcong was invading because it wanted to take over South Vietnam. But the Vietcong was evil, killing civilians—even women and children—and not even caring. The Vietcong used propaganda to make other South Vietnamese believe that all of this violence was the Americans' fault. But it wasn't; the Americans were trying to help us.

I probably didn't understand everything she said, but my mother cared enough to try to explain a very complex war to a six-year-old. I think she knew that although I didn't understand it at the time, eventually I would, so maybe I would remember that conversation. And I still do.

But as a child, I felt entirely confident that somehow we would win. We were the good guys, right? And the good guys had to win in the end. Kim Quy might finally come back, or maybe the Americans would help us stop the war.

However, I didn't know that the Vietcong had been around Cần Thơ for a while. I'm not sure how long, but they never took over until the president of South Vietnam surrendered on April 30, 1975. Men in uniforms I hadn't seen before invaded the streets, terrorizing the people. Má and Bà Nội made me stay in the house, and we tried to stay out of sight as much as possible.

"The war is over? Why aren't we going to the bunker?" I asked.

"Yes, son, it's over. Now be quiet," said Má. She didn't mention anything about the bunker.

Bà Nội looked at Má and said, "Remember what your husband said, Daughter. The Vietcong is taking over. You must hurry; take the children and leave for America."

Má didn't answer. Explosions and gunfire filled the silence. "No," she said. "I can't leave my husband."

"But your husband said you must leave. Take your identification and show it to the Americans. They will get you out of the country before it's too late," argued Bà Nội.

"But I cannot leave."

Bà Nội and Má argued until Chủ Sâu showed up at the bunker. "Má!" he said to Bà Nội, "It's time for you to leave! I can take you and the children to the Americans, but we have to go now."

"No," Bà Nội screamed over the noise of the explosions, "I will not leave the place where my husband is buried. I cannot leave him!" My uncle knew our culture. He knew that husbands and wives must be buried together, or they might be separated in death. There was no changing my grandmother's mind.

Artillery sounded outside, seeming to come closer and closer. "We have to go now!" I shouted, but no one appeared to hear me.

My uncle looked at my mother. "Then we must go—now. Gather the children," he said.

"I will not leave *my* husband either," said Má. "I don't even know if he's dead or alive. How could I live with myself if I left him here? How could I stand not knowing?"

Despite the explosions outside, the three of them continued to argue through the night, until their tempers began to fade. Slowly, they came to a silent agreement. Neither woman would leave. They would keep the family together. But my uncle left, fearing capture by the Vietcong.

We didn't have to wait much longer before my father came home—dressed in tatters and looking more haggard than I had ever seen him. I was shocked. My father had always dressed sharply, his uniform pristine.

My mother ran to him, hugging him tightly. He held her, asking her softly, "Why didn't you leave? Oh, why, why didn't you leave?" But he didn't seem that upset. He tried to smile at my mother and at us boys, but he just didn't seem to have the energy anymore.

"Where have you been? How did you get away? Have you seen your brothers?" Bà Nội and Má fired questions at him. I hovered around, and my father hugged me, and I asked him why he wasn't wearing his uniform. He said, "It's too dangerous now, Tuấn. We have lost South Vietnam, and the Vietcong has taken over. I can't wear it anymore." I wanted to ask more questions, but Má told me to go get Ba some water.

Ba didn't know where his brothers were, but he told us that most of the other South Vietnamese soldiers were already being held as prisoners of war. Fortunately, Ba's cousin, a communist, had told Ba to go home while he could. So he had walked home, but the Vietcong would be coming for him soon. I remember watching the adults around me, how Má and Bà Nội seemed to crumple under some invisible weight, and I knew at that moment that I had to take care of them. I was the man of the house.

Má then told me to go get food for Ba to eat, but for some reason, I was the only one who seemed hungry.

At some point that night, as I was trying to stay awake, Ba came to me and talked to me. I can't remember everything he said, but I do remember how he impressed upon me that I needed to be the man now. He said he might not be home anymore, but I wasn't sure what that meant. *Hadn't he always come back, even if he had been gone for months?* Though I didn't quite understand everything, I felt proud that my father thought I could do it, that I could take care of Má and Bà Nội.

That night, Ba and Má stayed awake all night, talking about their future and where we would go once Ba was taken away. I tried to stay awake to listen, but my eyelids drooped and eventually shut until morning.

The door of the house thudded, as if something was smashing against it. I startled awake, and Má gave a little scream. She and Ba were still over on their bed in the corner, looking as if they hadn't moved all night. I am not sure they had. But my father grabbed and held me, telling me that I must be brave, to be a big boy, and to take care of my mother and brothers. He said this over and over. Then he said goodbye to Má, who cried saying he couldn't go, shouldn't have to go. But he did. He opened the door, and the Vietcong took him, bundling him onto a truck. Má and Bà Nội screamed at the men not to take him. How could we survive without him?

Ignoring her questions, the Vietcong told my mother to bring my father some clothes to where he would be held at the local school. Where Ba would go after that, they couldn't say. But the soldiers said that they would send a letter to let Má know. I wanted to run to my father, but Má grabbed me and screamed at them, calling them inhuman and heartless. How could they take a little boy's father away in front of his eyes?

They took Ba anyway.

I hadn't *really* understood until that moment—the moment they dragged my father, so thin and dressed in rags, away into a truck—how grown up I would have to be. When the truck drove away, I found myself alone in Má's arms, tears making tracks in the dust on our faces.

CHAPTER THREE

MY MOTHER GATHERED UP CLOTHES and supplies for Ba and took them to him that night, asking the Vietcong again where they were taking my father. The Vietcong still didn't know, but they said that they would let him send a letter. I don't think she believed them.

Bà Nội'

Bà Nội decided to go talk to Ông Nội's brothers—the communist side of the family. She had to have known there was nothing they could do, but she wasn't giving her son up for dead. Her husband was the eldest of his brothers; they had to respect his family.

But that tradition had been before the war, and now, we had lost. Of course, Ông Nội's brothers said they couldn't do anything and then lectured her. "If your husband hadn't been so stubborn, so naïve, you would still have your sons," they reminded her, as if my grandmother had not suffered enough already.

Bà Nội's three eldest sons had all been taken away, and none of us knew where. I remember Bà Nội returning, numb and devastated. She looked at Má and said, "I know my husband would have scolded me for going to them. But what else can I do for my sons? Nothing. I had to try. The shame does not matter."

A short time after my father was taken away to the prison camp—a few days, maybe weeks—the Vietcong came to take everything we had. They told my mother that the next day they would be coming to kick us out of our house. We were allowed to take nothing from the house—we were allowed to take only what we were wearing.

When you are a child, your home stands as your place of safety, an untouchable base of love and security. All through the war—my father's absence, my grandfather's passing, all of the bombs and artillery—our house had withstood everything the world could throw at it. But without warning, in a matter of moments, the Vietcong ripped away my last shred of normalcy, and my childhood had come to an abrupt end. I learned later that just as many, if not more, civilians died at the hands of the Vietcong as had died during the war[1]. From what I saw after the war, I believe this to be true.

Looking back on it, I am sure Má and Bà Nội knew what was coming; at least, my father must have told Má, but I was six years old, a little boy tasked with being the man of the house in war-torn Vietnam. And I had just lost my whole world.

———

Má and Bà Nội moved us to the farm where my grandfather had planned to take us. Since my grandfather didn't have a chance to finish the repairs, the farm was in bad shape. In Cần Thơ, we had lived as respected middle-class citizens. Now, we were banished to a

Bà Nội'and grandkids

rundown farm, forced to live as outcasts, members of the losing side of a war—marked as trouble-makers and anti-nationalists. From that moment on, the course of our lives was changed. The prospects for my brothers' and my education had been restricted to grade school; we could never hold a public office; we could never better ourselves in Vietnam. Life itself was now a privilege we weren't guaranteed.

Ever since the Vietcong took my father away, my mother and Bà Nội were desperate for word of him. After a month or so of silence from the Vietcong, my mother went to what would be the equivalent of the county office and asked the Vietcong where her husband was being held. Again, they said they didn't know. "Just tell me! Just tell me if he's alive or dead! I just want to know," she screamed at them. They just sent her away, waving their AK-47s.

But my mother did not succumb to her grief. In our culture, we are taught that bad things happen. We pick ourselves up, and we go on. We fight for the people we love, and my mother had three little boys living in a wet, leaky house. She and Bà Nội worked to help repair the house with my uncle, Chú Út, who had moved with us. They searched for something, anything, that we could eat. We would find snail-like animals and small fish in the rice patty fields if we were lucky. But usually we just had rice.

I began to notice something. While everyone else became even skinnier than we were, Má's belly seemed to become more pronounced. And soon we all knew she was going to have a baby. Well, I am sure Bà Nội knew much sooner than we boys did, but it seemed like a ray of sunshine in this nightmare.

Then, the letter came. My mother and Bà Nội read and reread the letter that told them that my father was alive and imprisoned, and that we could go visit him. Immediately, my mother planned a visit and took me south with her, several hours by bus, to the camp where the Vietcong had imprisoned my father.

The last leg of our journey was by canoe through the marshes to where a few shacks rose out of the swamp. The buzz of insects and constant sloshing of the water seemed so unnatural to me, and now I can't even imagine what it must have been like for my father living there. His camp was one of over a dozen across South Vietnam that housed the Vietcong's prisoners. They called them "re-education camps," but in reality the camps existed purely to torture their occupants into submission. Day and night guards taunted their prisoners with the failure of the hated American and South Vietnamese military alliance.

Day after day, men were fed barely enough to stay alive—some rice porridge in the morning and broth at night—and were expected to perform more than a full day's work. Many men died as they combed the surrounding jungle and coastline for landmines. And just as many men, if not more, died from disease—with no access to modern medicine, their only remedies were from jungle plants. And the survivors' souls were weighed down with their own failures and the inevitability of death.

But I didn't quite understand the deadly nature of the prison my mother and I were visiting. I just knew that the place was not a good place, that it was a hard place in which to live. My mother had to have an idea of how bad it was going to be; of course she did. I began to understand my father's terrible condition the moment he met us beneath a simple bamboo shelter erected as a place for prisoners to receive visitors. The proud man in the pristine uniform was gone, replaced by a bone-thin man with bedraggled hair hanging around his dirty face. His guards hovered around us, making us afraid to speak to one another. But he held me tightly, and I felt, even if it was just for a moment, that everything would be okay.

My mother and father discussed some logistical things about the new house and how we were settling in, Má trying to make our lives at home sound better than they were. Seeing my father in this sickened state, we felt like our little dilapidated farm was a paradise. Ba said he didn't know when they would let him go, and Má looked at the ground, trying to hide her tears.

Before we left, Ba asked me if I was taking care of my mother, and I said I was. He said, "Good, she needs it now. You know? You have a little brother or sister coming." I nodded, attempting to appear more serious and grown up.

Soon we left the camp and began the exhausting journey back north to our farm. I watched Má stare out the bus window at the passing countryside and watched a tear fall from her eyes. She had wanted to see Ba more than anything else, but now she knew what she was leaving him to—a life of misery lived behind walls of barbed wire.

In the rural farmlands, time stood still. You could take a picture of a farmer in the rice fields and not know if it was from 1875 or 1975; traditions and culture remained untouched by the modern world. This sameness included the poverty of the farmland's people.

Rural Vietnam. We lived in a house similar to this

Every time I took my brothers out to find food or wandered through the house in the dark, I thought about our comfortable home in Cần Thơ. We may not have had money in abundance, but we had food to eat, a safe shelter with locking doors, and working lights.

In the fall, I had to go back to school. I begged Má and Bà Nội to let me stay home, to let me help them, but both women insisted that my education was too important. I didn't want to go to school anymore; none of my old friends, like Tam, would be at my new school here outside of the city. A new place, new people, and new neighborhood, all of these things frightened me.

For days leading up to my first day, I was so nervous that my stomach felt like it was twisting and rolling. The little food my mother was able to find for us didn't seem appealing. The lack of noises pressed in on me at night, making me feel that someone would come into our little house and attack us. My mother pretended she didn't notice how afraid I was, finding excuses to say positive things about my new school. When her plan didn't work, Má agreed to walk me to school on my first day.

When we lived in Cần Thơ, my morning walks to school with Ông Nội had been one of the best parts of the day. The many sights and smells around the market and time with Ông Nội now seemed like a fairy tale to me. But on this morning when we walked to my new school, Má led me through the small village, and though I had lived in the rural farmlands for months, it suddenly hit me how different this new world was—almost a totally different country.

The villagers ignored us, their bare feet squelching through the mud as they passed by. The trees swished and jungle sounds came through the brush, but otherwise, this place had no familiar sounds. The city had flooded the senses with every possible sound, taste, or smell all at once. It had been a comfort to me to know that so much was happening around me, as if I was safe being just one of many. But here, I stood out, practically a foreigner, a loser of the war.

My mother didn't seem to notice these things, or maybe she just ignored them, and she led me across a narrow bridge made of a single log and a narrow, flimsy rail for us to hold on to as we crossed. The bridge sagged under our weight, creaking horribly. When I complained, Má ordered me to hush. "Pay attention, Tuần," she said. "You know you have to walk home on your own."

Stricken, I paused. How would I find my way back? For the entire rest of the trip I focused on every single detail around me, trying to memorize the trees, that sagging house over there, the rice fields, anything that would help me get home.

After introducing me to my teacher, my mother kneeled down and told me that she would see me when I got home. I nodded, silent, as if my apprehension had stolen my words. After she left, the teacher looked down at me, eyes narrowed. "Sit," she snapped.

I think from that first moment, I knew she hated me. And I knew it was because of the war. Everything seemed to be about the war.

I sat a couple hours, trying to sit as still and silent as possible. Then the teacher let us out for recess. I sighed with relief. She hadn't called on me, spoken to me, or even really looked at me. But while the teacher may have been ignoring me, the other kids were under no such rule. That day, and every day after that, kids yelled at me, hit me, and called me a "child of a traitor." They called my father names, told me how stupid he was for working with the Americans, that he wouldn't be in prison if he had been smarter and had joined the communists.

After recess, the teacher began making snide remarks about those who did not support the communist party as she looked my way. I wanted to crawl under my seat, and I tried not to look ashamed because I wasn't, but then why did everyone have to make me feel so bad?

At half day, the kids my age were done with school, and the older kids would come and use the one room school house for the second half of the day. I had never been so thankful to leave school. I ran home, just ran. Down the path, over the bridge, and through the village to our farm. I know it was several miles, but I felt like I flew through it all. At home, I finally felt safe.

But the next day, no matter how much I begged, my mother still insisted that I had to go to school. I did, and got into a fight at school. The next day the kids yelled at me again, swore at me, and called my family all manner of disgusting names. The day after that, when I got to the flimsy bridge, I saw the water and had an idea. I didn't care how disgusting the water looked; I jumped in. I ran back home and told Má that I had fallen in. She didn't believe me and made me change and go back to school. Day after day, I had to go back to that school and face the other kids. Even children seemed to understand that I was now less than human in the eyes of the new government. A person without a country.

After my sister Loan was born, Bà Ngoại, my maternal grandmother, talked to Bà Nội and Má; the way they talked, I knew it must be serious. After the three women had their meeting, Má came to talk to us boys.

"Sons," she said, "What do you think about moving closer to your maternal grandmother? Would you like that?"

We knew this wasn't actually a request for our opinion, so we just nodded. Má smiled. "Good. We will leave soon."

I learned later that Má knew she was going to have to find a way to provide for our family, so she had taken up buying and selling rice illegally to make money. But she had to leave us for days at a time, so she need more help with us kids. Maternal grandmother was so worried, she offered to help us move closer to her village so she could keep an eye on us. Bà Nội paid for material so Má's brothers could build us a small house, a shack really, for us to live in. This time, when we were in need, our family gathered around us to help.

―――――――――――――――

Má, my siblings, and I moved to the small shack about a month after my sister was born. This village was even smaller than the village where we had lived with Bà Nội. But at least I had a different school.

When we first got to the village, there really was no school to speak of. I was excited that I may not have to face horrible children like at my last school. But the community got together to make a one room schoolhouse of bamboo with large leaves for a roof.

When I first started at this new school, I was afraid that I would be tormented for my father's involvement in the war, but I slowly realized that these kids didn't know or didn't care that much about my family history. For the first time since we left Cần Thơ, I had friends.

My family settled into a routine. Má would leave for a few days, and I would take care of my younger brothers and sister as best I could. I didn't know anything about babies, but Bà Ngoại taught me what she could when Má was away. I soon learned that Loan didn't cry so much when she was fed. But when food is scarce, feeding her wasn't always an option. I marked time by counting and recounting the days when my mother was gone, always waiting for her to come back—worried she wouldn't come back at all.

One evening when my mother was home, we were gathering around the front of our shack to eat our dinner, bits of rice my mother had saved, when we saw someone coming towards us. I felt a sudden wave of fear when I saw it was a man. Would he steal our food? Would he hurt us? My mother cried out, but instead of running away or telling us to go inside, she ran to the man. By the time she had her arms around the man's neck, I recognized him. It was my father.

My brothers and I ran to him, wrapping our arms around whatever part of him we could reach, his waist, his legs, just to feel him—to see if he was for real. After a moment of our joyous reunion, Ba said, "Where is the baby?"

Má smiled and led him back to the house. That's when Ba saw her, his baby girl, for the first time. "This is Loan, your daughter," said Má.

Ba had tears in his eyes as he cradled his little girl, the only daughter he would ever have. Not until I held my own little girl did I understand the instant bond that he must have been feeling. Boys are tougher, more resilient. He loved us boys dearly, but Loan was his princess.

CHAPTER FOUR

I LEARNED LATER THAT ÔNG Nội's brothers, who were members of the communist party, had used their connections within the party to get my father released from prison. Though that might sound generous of them, they really just wanted to free themselves of the shame of having nephews in prison. In the months after my father's release, Ông Nội's brothers eventually got all my uncles released.

Though released from the prison camp, their freedom was only an illusion, and the communists enjoyed showing up at our doorstep without notice to take my father back to prison. They said this was part of his parole, and he needed to be reminded of the "lessons" that they had taught him during that first year when he was in prison. But the Vietcong actually wanted to remind us that our home wasn't really ours; they could show up at any time, take everything away, and throw us in prison. We lived in constant fear, knowing that if the worst happened we would be able to do nothing except cry in sorrow.

Every time the Vietcong showed up at our door, we never knew how long they were taking Ba. At first they came every week, having him work on roads or other types of manual labor. As time passed, the Vietcong came less often, but they always eventually came back to take Ba away again. The times when Ba was gone were the hardest for everyone, and Má still had to make trips up the river to distant farms to buy rice to sell on the

A patty field in rural Vietnam

black market. Ba helped her with that when he could, but otherwise she had to make the trips alone.

When Má left, I took care of my siblings. As an eight-year-old, I knew where to find snails in the rice patty fields and which pools of water would catch stranded fish. We ate anything we could find, often crawling through marshes and coming home covered in a thick mud. One time, I sent Trường and Phong out to find food while I took care of Loan. They came back laughing, and when I went outside, I found them crowded around a bowl covered in large leaves.

"What did you find?" I asked.

"It's an eel," said Trường.

Excited for a chance to eat some meat, I pulled back the leaves, and a black head rose out of the bowl. I jumped back and yelled at Trường, "You idiot! It's a cobra!"

Somehow we managed to cut the snake's head off without getting hurt, and we ate the snake for dinner. I decided snake didn't taste as good as eel.

_____

In 1978, when I was nine, my brother An was born. He always seemed to be crying, and there was never enough milk to keep him quiet. Ma taught me how to boil rice and use the water, what now is called rice milk, to feed him. But eventually the rice too would run out, and I wasn't able to feed him. Each time my father left with the Vietcong, he would tell me that I was the man of house while he was gone. I had to take care of my brothers and sister.

One time my mother left, saying that she should be gone for only a couple days. But after two days, she wasn't home. After about six days, I was out of the food that we had in the house. That night, An screamed desperately. I tried to rock him and let him know that he was okay, but he just kept crying. Ma always reminded me that we had a distant cousin, Di Út, in the village who would help us if things got too desperate. I thought, *She has a baby and feeds her. Maybe she would feed An too.*

I didn't want to face the darkness, a blackness that made you feel as though you had gone blind, but I had to toughen up. My dad had never stopped telling me that when he was gone, I was the man of the house. I couldn't let him down. So Loan, Phong, and Trường left with me for Di Út's house. Trường carried a torch to cut the stifling darkness. Every time I had to leave the house at night, I wished for the electricity that had been so abundant in the city. But we made do; we had no choice.

When we reached the house, An was still screaming, crinkling face red and puffy. The neighbor must have heard us coming; An's wailing made that easy. When we reached her, she reached out for An and rocked him. "How long has your mother been gone this time?" she asked.

"I'm not sure. She was supposed to be back by now," I said.

Our neighbor looked at An. "Oh, he's starving. Let me feed him," she said. "Now come inside. All of you." We shuffled into her house, and she asked, "Have you children eaten?"

"Yes," I said.

Loan cut in, "But we're still hungry."

I felt a little embarrassed, but the woman looked at us and said, "Well, I have some leftovers from dinner. Why don't you go eat it? I was going to have it for breakfast, but you go ahead and have it."

I felt that some sort of miracle had just occurred: the four of us older children eating rice and some bits of fish. It seemed like the most heavenly thing to me at the time. After we had eaten, our neighbor looked at me and whispered softly, "If you bring him back to me in the morning, I will feed him again. No need for him to get hoarse from all that crying."

I cannot describe the relief I felt at that moment. My little brother wasn't going to die. It would be okay. The Vietcong tried to take away our lives, our spirit—our very humanity—but it failed. People like this woman still showed kindness, still gave us hope. And it's that hope that got us through.

When my mom returned a day or two later, we learned that the Vietcong had caught her trying to buy and sell rice on the black market. They had put her in jail for a week. As soon as she got home, she reached for An, crying over him when she found out that he was alive. He was a survivor too.

Since I had become the primary caretaker of my siblings, I worried about finding them food to eat, keeping them clean, and making sure that they all stayed safe. I loved them dearly, but I was a kid, and sometimes I just wanted a break. For me, that meant school. At the school in Bà Ngoại's village, I had made friends, and we played marbles, practiced our self-defense moves, and got in trouble—like most boys do.

Early on, we would steal giant grapefruit from the master at the martial arts school. Being crippled, the man could only shout at us, swearing that we would get our comeuppance. The boys and I just laughed and kicked the giant grapefruit around like a soccer ball, holding game after game until the fruit fell apart.

Although we loved our games, we had our eyes on something else—we wanted to study martial arts. This particular martial arts master was well known in our region of Vietnam. People brought their sons from all around the region.

Ba had taught me a few basic self-defense moves, but I told him that I wanted to study with the master. So he talked to the master's son-in-law and got me an interview with the master. At the agreed time, Ba took me to the master's house where Ba presented him a gift of spirits. After they had chatted for a while over tea, the master called me over. He stared at every inch of my frame and asked me pointed questions, determining if I had what it takes. I tried to look tough, like I could take whatever he threw at me.

"Have the boy come back with a rooster and a bottle of spirits. These offerings will be presented to my ancestors. If they accept him, he can learn here," said the master.

I returned a few days later to present my gifts. The rooster was to be cooked and presented with half of the alcohol to the master's ancestors. I remember looking for a sign that the ancestors were accepting me as a student, but I didn't see one. However, the master said they had accepted me.

Every evening after I had put my siblings to bed, I would run over to the master's house and practice the moves that I had been taught. When the master called me in, I had to perform the moves to his satisfaction, or be beaten as punishment. I didn't see this as cruelty, but just as part of the rigorous program, always thankful that I had been chosen.

My knuckles bled and my body ached, bruising all over. But the alcohol I had brought would be mixed with herbs and poured on my cuts and bruises, numbing them. In the midst of the stresses life threw at me, going to the master's house was a solace.

I came home one night to find Chủ Út, now a communist, talking with my parents over tea. "We have to get a boat. If we got a boat, we could sail to Thailand and escape the Vietcong," said Ba.

"That would be impossible. Where would you get the boat? You don't have money," said Chủ Út. "And even if you did manage to get a boat, how would you keep the Vietcong from taking it away? They see everything. And the pirates. You know pirates now infest the sea. You know what they do to Vietnamese refugees."

"The Vietcong are not the only one who sees," broke in Má, and she looked my way. "Silence. Do not talk about these things. Not in front of Tuần and the other children."

Escape? Was that possible? The Americans had fled after the war, but now escaping seemed impossible. Of course, there had been rumors of people leaving, but not many about refugees surviving the journey. At the time I assumed that my parents were just indulging in wishful thinking. This was our life. We should just accept and deal with it.

Around the time I became distracted with my martial arts, my father and his brothers Chủ Bảy and Chủ Sâu began working on an old boat. It looked like it had been through a war—which, of course, it had. To explain away why they had a boat, which looked suspicious to the Vietcong, Ba and my uncles said that they wanted to start a business carrying fruits and vegetables to the market, and they began to try to obtain the proper permits from the government.

People that I didn't know came to the house and had discussions with my father in hushed tones, making me wonder what on earth they would want with Ba's old boat. Maybe he was going to try to sell it to make a profit?

Finally, the boat was finished, sailable at least. After dark, Ba, my uncles, and I took the boat for a test run. Back at the house, we celebrated the start of the new business. I thought that this might be the change my family needed for a better future.

But there was a knock at the door. The Vietcong had come. "We have been told that you have a boat, a boat you plan on using to escape Vietnam!" they shouted.

"No, no, we plan on starting a new business to transport cargo to the market," said Ba. "See? Here are the permits."

"We have heard from various sources to the contrary," said the officer. "So as far as we are concerned, you are planning on exiting the country. However, if you wish to refute this claim, you have a month to do so. But we are confiscating the boat, pending this investigation."

Ba and my uncles knew that there was no arguing. They could easily go to jail at this officer's whim.

They never did go try to get their boat back. And I learned later why. They were guilty. Of course, they were trying to escape. That had been the whole plan. Buy the boat, fix it up, and flee to Thailand.

Ba and my uncles seemed devastated, but they didn't give up.

About a year later in 1982, Chủ Út used his communist contacts to help Chủ Sâu escape to Malaysia and, eventually, to America. And he survived—one of the few that did.

In 1983, I started high school in a small city nearby. This meant a longer commute, harder work, and more kids my age. It also meant more exposure to the Vietcong.

One day when I was leaving school, I heard someone yelling over a loudspeaker somewhere down the street. Walking that way, I could make out, "These men are spies for the Americans and will be executed one week from today because of their crimes!" The Vietcong repeated this message over and over, declaring the sovereignty of the communist party and the inferiority of anyone who opposed them.

One week later, hundreds of people gathered around the soccer field of the school to see the five men being executed. The men stood on a stage, each tied to a pole. The men's families stood by, screaming for their loved one's release. But the Vietcong ignored them, tying the prisoners to stakes—torso, head, and legs firmly secured with tight ropes.

The Vietcong soldiers held AK-47s and faced both the prisoners and the crowd, ensuring that no escape or rescue attempts could succeed.

"These men, formerly of the South Vietnamese Army, are American spies and enemies of the communist party. They are being executed for their crimes," shouted an officer through his bullhorn. He turned to the tied prisoners. "Any last words?"

The prisoners shouted, their words overlapping one another in a cacophony of sound: "Long live South Vietnam!" "The Vietcong are animals!" 'Their leader lies! Death to Ho Chi Minh!"

The Vietcong emptied their magazines into the prisoners, blowing them apart beyond recognition.

Although my family had suffered, and I had heard of the atrocities of the Vietcong, I never experienced first-hand the pure hatred and inhumanity that governed the communists. We, the Southern Vietnamese, were nothing to them—less than human. We were sand in their eyes.

The home that I had once known would never be coming back; there would be no rescue. My family no longer had a safe place in this country. We were a hated people in a foreign land.

———

When I was fourteen, Má had been making the rice runs up the river for almost eight years. Every time she left, I worried that she wouldn't come back. But I was fourteen now, practically a man, so I should be able to do something—anything—to make sure my mother came back home. The next time Má prepared to go upriver, I went up to her and said, "Má, I want to go with you this time."

"No, Tuần. You must stay to take care of your brothers and sister," she said.

"But Trường is old enough to take care of them by himself," I said. "So I am going with you this time."

"No, he's not old enough."

"He's older than I was when I started to take care of everyone."

Má looked at me, looking at my face as if that would tell her what to decide. It must have because she said, "Okay. You can come."

We left that night, paddling against the current. Since the fall of Saigon, the Vietcong had become all too aware of the illegal traders making use of the river. They knew our trade routes, but we had no choice.

On our way out to the secluded village Má had chosen, I asked her why we had to go so far to buy our rice. There were plenty of villages closer that were secluded. Má explained that few illegal rice buyers went so far out, so we would be able to make more money—buy more rice—if we went farther out. This entire trip would make us the equivalent of five to seven U.S. dollars.

When we reached the village in the afternoon, their living conditions astonished me. Their little huts made our house look like our nice house in Cần Thơ. The village was so small, we hoped that they would have enough rice for us to buy so we wouldn't have to go to another village. My mother was a tough woman, but I couldn't even imagine how she had been doing these trips by herself for so many years. Despite our worries, the villagers were all too happy to sell us their rice. Apparently, they hadn't seen a rice trader in a while, because by the time we loaded the rice into our little boat, we were in danger of being submerged.

Ma didn't want to start back during the day.

At first I didn't understand. "How can we see where we're going if we don't leave while we still have daylight?" I asked.

She explained that the Vietcong knew that people used the waterways to transport items for the black market. It wasn't safe to travel during the day. We rested for a few hours and prepared to leave that night. When she and I got into the boat with the rice, the boat sunk even further. "Má, we are going to sink!" I said.

"Tuấn! Shut up! Just paddle—quietly. Do not make a sound. The Vietcong has checkpoints along the river," she said.

We paddled, trying to be as quiet as possible. The night was so black, so dark without electricity; we had only the moon and stars to guide us, but they were often covered by trees and other vegetation. Fear gripped my body, making it hard for me to paddle without shaking. I accidentally made a loud splashing noise with my paddle, and Má hissed at me. For the first time, I recognized fear in her voice.

I tried to block out the fear, the negative thoughts. *We are going to get caught. They are going to kill us.* But I had to just keep paddling. Then a voice came from the darkness followed by a small light: "Stop! Land the canoe, or we will shoot!"

"Keep paddling, Tuần!" Má said. I did, but I was terrified. "Get past the bridge! That's the county line. Then we're almost home!" she said.

We paddled as fast as we could after two nights of fighting the river. Shots rang out around us, but we weren't hit. The Vietcong continued to yell and shoot at us, but we kept paddling. The bridge came in sight, and passed us overhead. We heard stamping on the bridge above us and water splashing on all sides. They were so close now, shooting down at us from the bridge. Surely they would hit us.

We sped away from the bridge, but there was splashing, the boat jerked, and we hit the shore. Vietcong soldiers surrounded us, one man jumping into the boat, telling us to get out of the boat or they would shoot us. He slapped Má, yelling, "Why didn't you stop? Why didn't you stop?"

The man holding Má shook her and yelled in her face. I still held my paddle, and I stepped forward to help her. A man raised his gun at me. "Put it down," he said. "Do it. Do it now." I put the paddle down.

They took all of our rice, but Má begged them not to. "Please don't take all of it! What will I feed my children?"

A communist swore at her and said he didn't care if she fed them or not. He didn't care if we died. If she wanted any of it, she would have to go ask the authorities for permission to get some back.

They let us go, and once the fear faded enough, I felt frustrated with myself. *I should have been more careful with that paddle! I shouldn't have let it splash.* Má cried the entire way back to our house. As I watched her, I couldn't believe that she had been doing this by herself. How was it even possible? I knew we had been lucky that the Vietcong had let us go. Má told me later that she got caught fairly often, but she didn't always have so much rice to lose.

I had always respected my mother, but after that trip up river, I respected her like a hero, a woman who fought to take care of her children. Children she loved.

Trường, Phnoe, Bich, and Tuần (Chuck) 2nd row: Bà Nội, Thiem Bảy and My Den

In April 1984, we celebrated my maternal grandfather's death anniversary, and my mother's family gathered at Bà Ngoại's house. We feasted, and for once our bellies were full and satisfied. We kids laughed and joked around in a way that was rare. It was as if our troubles had disappeared. A photographer happened to be wandering through the village and asked to take our pictures. We so rarely got to have our pictures taken that I remember it was a special novelty to be photographed.

When I look at those pictures now, it's hard to believe that someone captured our faces the night before the biggest journey of my life was to begin.

Chun Bay, Duong Bay, Can Ut, Ba, Duong Tu, Can Tam

Di Bay (Má's Sister), Di Tu (Má's older sister), Má, Chi Tuyen (Di Tu's daughter), Mo Tam (Má's sister-in-law), Mo Út (Má's sister-in-law)

The next morning my parents woke my siblings and me, telling us that we were going to visit Chủ Út in Gach Gai. Gach Gai was a small city on the coast of Vietnam, and I had never been there before. To go anywhere in Vietnam required a permit from your local government that mandated you to check in at your destination. The permit was good only for specific dates, so you had to return at the appointed time, or you would be arrested for traveling illegally.

Before we left, Ba took me aside and confirmed what I already suspected—we were leaving Vietnam. Before we could cross the sea, we had to travel to the lower left coast of Vietnam. Ba impressed upon me the danger we were about to face, but I had to remain strong for the family. He was counting on me.

We all got in a boat, and Ba added a few containers of diesel fuel, much more than we needed to go to Gach Gai. When I asked Ba about the extra fuel, he said that Chủ Út had told him that fuel was much more expensive in Gach Gai, so we could make a profit if we brought some diesel down to sell. After my recent trip with Má to buy and sell rice, I understood that this seemed an easier way to make some money, but I also guessed that it must be illegal. So I decided not to ask about anything else.

In Vietnam, the rivers and channels around the southern delta were like roads and highways; just as many people traveled by boat as they did by land. It was common for a Vietnamese family to be traveling this way, so I hoped that we wouldn't be stopped.

After my experience with Má, I understood the danger that we were in, and my mind kept replaying our flight down the river, the Vietcong yelling and shooting at us. Throughout the day I watched Ba and Má, the stress etched in their faces.

"How much farther?" the little kids whined.

"Not much farther," said Ba. "Just a couple of hours."

Má passed around food, but with my stomach knotted with anxiety, I couldn't eat the food offered to me. An hour later, the Vietcong stopped us. One of them pointed at the fuel. "Why do you have so much fuel? You are trying to escape!"

"No!" said Ba. "My brother said I could make some money by selling the fuel down in Gach Gai. See? Here are our permits to go to Gach Gai for my father's death anniversary. I thought I could make some money since I am already going down there."

The soldier looked over the permits and didn't seem able to disagree with them, but then he looked again at the containers of fuel. "These papers are in order, but that does not permit you to carry so much fuel. I am sure you know people are trying to leave, especially from Gach Gai." He paused and looked at the rag tag group in the old boat. "So we will hold this fuel until you return. When you travel back up to your home village, we will return these to you."

Ba didn't even try to protest. I am sure his mind must be on his several trips to prison. One word could send him back there, and he never knew when, or if, he would get out. So he agreed, and the Vietcong sent us on our way.

We had been lucky. They took our fuel instead of our freedom. I thought that was a decent trade.

When we reached Gach Gai, Ba didn't take us to Chủ Út's house; he took us to Chủ Bảy's in-law's house. "Why are we here, Ba?" I asked.

"We are here for Ông Nội's death anniversary. You know that," Ba said.

I knew not to say anything, and I wondered what was going on, but I figured the adults must have just decided to move the cel-

Chủ, Tien Út, and their kids

ebration. After dinner, the adults gathered around over tea and began to talk. Ba explained to Chủ Bảy and the other adults how he had lost the fuel.

"Yes, you were lucky," said Chủ Bảy. "You could have been taken to prison."

"But what do we do now for fuel?" said Ba. "We can't make it to Malaysia now; we may not even be able to make it to Thailand."

Malaysia? Thailand?

"We can buy more fuel," said Chủ Bảy.

"How? If we buy that much fuel at once, we will be arrested almost immediately," said Ba.

"We'll send out everyone to each buy what fuel they can find, and no one person will buy enough for the Vietcong to take notice," said Chủ Bảy. "We won't find enough to get to Malaysia, but we could get to Thailand."

We were going to Thailand. We were escaping.

They had sent the other kids to bed, but I was fifteen; they treated me like an adult now. I remember feeling so proud that I knew what was going on before the other kids. For the rest of the night, the adults laid out the plans for our escape. As they finalized the plans, I remembered the stories I had heard of people trying to escape Vietnam. Fear gripped me and didn't let go.

The next day everyone gathered supplies. The men went around the city buying fuel, and Má and my aunt, Thiem Bảy', went and bought food for the journey. The Vietcong might have been suspicious at the amount of food the women were buying, but the permits Má had for the death anniversary covered any of the questions posed by the authorities. Ba, Chủ Bảy, and Chủ Út buried the fuel by the beach so that no one would see that they had such a large amount.

That night I lay awake in bed, thinking of all of the horrible stories that I had heard over the years—people dying in horrendous ways as they tried to escape an almost equally horrendous way of life. Ba and Má knew that we had a small chance of surviving, but that small chance looked better than what our life would be if we remained in Vietnam. Over and over I rolled around the possibilities in my mind. We had to escape; we had to leave—or at least try.

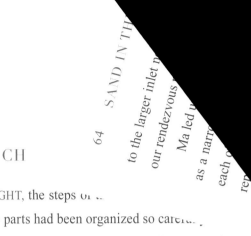
CH

I LAY AWAKE ALL NIGHT, the steps oı ᴄᴄ

my mind. Each of these parts had been organized so carᴄᴜᴜ ,

had my parents been planning this? The night hung silent around me, my

four siblings were quiet, deep in sleep. But I couldn't sleep, and the hours

ticked by until my mother shook me, saying, "Tuần, it's time to get up."

"What time—" I began to ask, but she cut me off.

"2:30," she said. "Now get up. It's time to leave. Your father has gone

ahead as planned, and now we have to leave."

I stumbled up off the floor to the water barrel out back. I washed my

face and stared into the water, deep and black. I tried to imagine our little

boat adrift in miles and miles of water, but I couldn't. We had to cross the

ocean. The thought both thrilled and terrified me. Since we had planned

on leaving so early, we had said our goodbyes to our distant relatives last

night, thanking them for their kindness. I had felt like we were saying

goodbye to every family member, every distant loved one that I didn't

have a chance to wish farewell.

Má shook awake each of my siblings and sent them to the water bar-

rel, and they brushed their teeth. Leaving me in charge, Má took our few

belongings and the water containers to the little boat, coming back splat-

tered with mud. Má ushered us outside into the darkness, quieting any

worries from us. We reached the shore of the channel that would lead us ear the ocean. Closer to the inlet, we would arrive at

point where Ba should be waiting for us.

s down the bank to a log set firmly into the mud that served

w gangplank to a boat that was similar to a canoe. Carefully,

f us climbed into the small boat that looked old and needed some

airs, but we all managed to get inside. Má told Phong, Loan, and An

to get into the bottom of the canoe. Trường and I pushed the boat further into the water, climbing in at the last minute. As we pushed our boat through the water with long poles, the early-morning blackness cloaked us from the Vietcong. But we couldn't see anything either. The channel was shallow and with so many people in the boat, I feared that we would run aground or get stuck on the foliage in the water.

Without warning, a light shown from a house on the shore. We had been told that communists inhabited certain houses along the shore, and I felt terrified that someone might catch sight of us moving through the channel. An old man walked onto the porch of the house, but he didn't appear to see us.

My brother and I tried to move our poles quietly, since any noise created yet another chance of discovery. I once again remembered the gun fire that had shot through the dark as the Vietcong chased Má and me down the river. My arms felt stiff with fear. We had only a couple hours from the time that we left to make it to the meeting place; we had to be there before the dawn. I looked into the water, but I could see only darkness.

The weeds became so thick that the boat barely moved forward. Má told Trường and I to get into the water and push the boat through the water from behind. Without saying a word, we dropped over the side of the boat. Our feet hit the bottom of the channel, mud oozing between our toes. As we pushed the boat, we put much of our effort into making as little sound as possible. Má tried to help us by guiding the boat with the long pole, but she had to make sure that the little ones didn't cry. Our skin became wrinkled, and silt gathered between our skin and our clothes. Long water weeds tangled in our legs, slimy and startling.

Suddenly a bark sounded through the darkness; a dog ran on the bank of the channel, barking furiously. Má tried to send it away, waving her pole at the dog's face. The beast kept barking, the sound ringing through the dark. Má shoved the stick at Phong, grabbed some of our food from her bag, and threw it at the dog on the bank. Immediately the dog stopped its persistent barking and ran after the food, giving us a chance to disappear into the darkness.

"Hurry, Tuần, Trường," she said. "Someone might have heard that."

Despite our best efforts, the boat still didn't move fast enough. With every passing moment, the sky grew lighter and lighter. My father's voice rang through my head with the message he had given me the night before: "Tuần, you must make sure that your mother, brothers, and sister make it to the meeting place. If any of us don't make it there on time, we can't risk the others getting caught."

"We'll leave them behind?" I asked.

He nodded. "Yes, Tuần, so you must make sure our family is there on time. I am trusting you." Over and over Ba's words swirled in my head, my chest tightening with a cold fear; I was failing him.

Suddenly Trường's head fell beneath the water's surface. Then my feet didn't hit the bottom of the channel, and I sank below the water. Kicking out I found the bottom of the channel and pushed up. Breaking the surface, I gasped for air, trying to alleviate the tightness in my chest.

"What are you doing?" hissed Má.

"The ground—it's gone!" I spluttered.

"Noise! No noise!" she said.

Trường and I swam back to the boat, trying to push with our hands and kick with our feet, but the boat didn't move much. Finally, Má called for us to get back in the boat, and we took the poles back up and began pushing us forward again.

The water became more maneuverable as we got closer to the ocean. As we moved faster through the water we raced the ever brightening sky. "There! The boat!" said Má, startling me out of my focus. "Tuấn, move the boat to the side. I don't see the signal."

As we moved to the side of the channel, Má scanned the horizon for any sign of other boats, and for any sign of the signal.

"Why can't we go to the boat?" asked Trường.

"We need to wait for the signal from your father. He will let us know when it's safe."

Ba had told us that the Vietcong might find the fuel or the waiting boat and create a trap for us. He would make sure that it was safe for us to approach the boat. We sat, watching the shore below the gray sky until finally catching sight of a small flame, like one from a cigarette lighter.

"That's the signal!" whispered Má.

Slowly we paddled over to the boat, and I kept looking around, thinking that this can't be it. The boat was barely more than a large canoe—great for carrying produce, but far from being anything ocean worthy. Near the back of the boat sat two motors: a larger outboard motor and a smaller trolling motor attached to a long shaft. Our lives depended on these two motors that had to propel us across the ocean. Each of us climbed into the boat, the kids lying in the bottom under tarps.

Eighteen of us gathered in the boat that day. The seven in my family, the six in Chủ Bảy's family, and my mother's brother in law Đường Bảy and his daughter, Bến, made up most of our party. But to my mother's disapproval, Chủ Bảy brought an acquaintance of his. Apparently Chủ Bảy had been drinking with this friend and had let it slip that he and his family were escaping. His friend had told him that he had to go with Chủ Bảy or he would tell the authorities they were trying to leave. Of course Chủ Bảy agreed to take him. The other two passengers were a man named Bác Hai and his son; they had paid my father to be able to come along.

"Sink the other boats," said Ba. "We can't have the Vietcong noticing that we have left the country. We must leave no trace." Chủ Bảy and Đường Bảy chopped holes in the other boats to sink them and pushed us into the water.

With so many people in the barely sea-worthy boat, in addition to supplies, the boat seemed to sink too low in the water. Despite our fear, we tried to huddle low, not making a sound. The morning was quiet and stifling. Slowly we made our way from the shore, the adults scanning the horizon for signs of the Vietcong. "A boat!" someone hissed, and everyone sunk even lower. At first we thought we had been found out, but the boat passed without noticing us. "Just a fisherman," echoed around the boat.

We continued forward, heading west to freedom. "How do we know where we are going?" I whispered to Ba.

"Bác Hai was a captain in the South Vietnamese Army, so he knows how to navigate," he said.

"How?"

"The stars," said Ba, pointing to the sky. "And his compass. We are fortunate that we found him. He's how we are going to find our way to Thailand."

"But I thought Chủ Sâu said that Thailand wasn't taking many more refugees?"

"They're not," he said. "But that's all we have fuel for. We'll have to risk it."

I didn't know what to say after that. We sat in nervous silence, listening to the loud noise of the motor. Chủ Bảy pushed the motor to go as fast as he could without overdoing it. We had to get out of Vietcong waters as quickly as possible. We had begun to leave the sight of the shore behind when the motor suddenly stopped, leaving us adrift.

Ba and Chủ Bảy took turns pulling the motor cord over and over. Má whispered for Buddha to save us, to get us out of Vietcong waters. Đường Bảy tried to keep us moving forward with the trolling motor, but it was painfully slow.

"Tuần!" said Ba. "Come hold this flashlight while Chủ Bảy and I work on the motor!"

I ran over and held the flashlight, looking around the boat. The children slept peacefully in the bottom of the boat, unaware of the danger around them. Má was making a sail out of a tarp while Chủ Bảy's wife, Thiem Bảy, prayed.

"Tuần! Light!" scolded Ba. I had gotten distracted and wasn't holding the light properly.

"Hold the light straight! We have to get this motor running or we will be found. They *will* kill us. Do you understand?" he said.

I flinched and held the light back on the motor. Frustrated, Ba left and gave Chủ Bảy the chance to work on the motor.

"Tuần, he's worried. You know that, right?" said Chủ Bảy. "We were hoping to be out of Vietcong waters by now, but everything has gone wrong."

I knew my uncle was right, but then why didn't I feel any better?"

Ba and Chủ Bảy pulled the engine cord over and over, and Ba told Chủ Bảy to clean the motor's filter to make sure it wasn't blocked. Finally, the motor caught, and scattered quiet cheers sounded across the boat. Everyone relaxed as we headed away from the Vietcong towards the safety across the ocean.

I must have fallen asleep because I awoke several hours later in the middle of the day, the light shining down on my head. "Má? Ba?" I said, confused.

"We ran out of fuel," said Ba.

"Bác Hai, where are we? Are we out of Vietcong waters?" asked Má.

Bác Hai looked at his compass, somehow calibrating our location. "I think we are just past the border of Vietcong territory. But we could drift back if we don't move forward soon," he said.

The adults were silent for a moment. "If they find us now," began Má, but she didn't finish. We knew what would happen; the Vietcong would kill us.

Má and Thiem Bảy continued to pray for awhile, but as the sun rose, everyone grew quiet under the relentless sun. Má rationed the water, giving most of it to the little kids.

Quiet hour passed after quiet hour, the only sound coming from the waves sloshing against the side of the boat. The sun stole most of the moisture in the air, leaving behind the salt to chafe against my skin. The sway of the boat wreaked havoc on my stomach, which at least took the edge off my hunger. As my skin grew pink and inflamed, I leaned into a wind that wasn't there, as if begging nature for relief. But wind never blew against my face. The boat didn't move. The makeshift sail that Má had constructed out of the tarp acted as our only shade, which you could barely see under the kids crowded into it.

Finally the sun grew tired, falling slowly from the sky. The wind, as if sensing its jailer's inattention, began to pick up, bringing cool relief and the taste of hope. We could do this now. We could beat this. Bác Hai checked the signs, invisible to my eyes, to see how much we had drifted in the ocean. Compass in hand, he stood up in the boat and paused. "We seem to be drifting towards Thailand," he said.

But with the wind came the waves. Higher and higher they rolled, sending our boat up, then crashing back down. Water roared into the boat, a little at first, then more and more, until we realized that we had to bail out the boat or we would sink.

The boat almost capsized, but we somehow stayed afloat. The adults shouted at one another and grabbed anything, everything we had that could hold water. No words can describe the terror that followed as we battled the watery darkness, always afraid that the old boat would fall apart or flip over. Wave after wave came. Our limbs grew clammy and wrinkled as we moved in a mechanical motion to keep our boat from sinking beneath the waves. The children cried until they grew hoarse and sniffled in terror through the water. Hour after hour passed in this way, and as each hour passed, I became more sure that we would die, drowned in the sea. When I became numb to all feeling, I saw gray light appear at the edges of the endless ocean.

Finally the sun had returned, calming the wind and sending the waves on their way. Several inches of water remained in the bottom of the boat, but we didn't care. We fell asleep exhausted. I awoke to the sun high in the sky. Salt caked on my skin, flaking as I moved. People around me began to wake too, and the adults assessed the situation. Our food, the rice that we had brought, had become soggy with salt water. "What will we eat?" I asked.

"We will eat this, Tuần. The rice is all we have," said Má.

We choked down some of the half-cooked food, the rice crunching in our mouths. We had about half a quart of water left, which gave each of the little kids a mouthful. If we didn't get discovered soon, or if it didn't rain, the smallest kids might suffer from heatstroke or die from dehydration. I felt as if I had to do something, but I was as helpless as my parents.

During the second day under the beating sun, someone continually kept a look out for ships. After the fall of Saigon, humanitarian organizations from around the world sent rescue ships to pick up refugees from Vietnam. Even ten years after the end of the war, people still fled Vietnam by the thousands. There was a saying that if a light pole could have left Vietnam, it would have.

We prayed that one of these ships would find us. The alternative was the Vietcong or Thai pirates, former fishermen who now made a living taking advantage of refugees. With either of the last two options, we could be dead, so we prayed not just for a ship, but for the right ship.

Those who weren't looking for a ship laid down in pure misery. By sundown the water was almost gone, and we were totally out of food. Although we all felt relief from the heat, fear rippled through us. We now had to face the ocean. I looked around at the adults and could see the raw fear and exhaustion on their faces.

They were certain that this was the last night that they could face the dark waves. But tonight they would fight, and tonight they would win. We bailed out the boat, over and over, wave after rolling wave. At one point Đường Bảy cried out, sounding as if he was crying. His voice cracked with sorrow and fear. "How could I have brought my daughter into this? She will die. I will die!"

Ba looked at him, anger twisting his face. "Look at my family. My brother's family. Our entire families are here in this boat. If this boat flips we all die. At least your wife and your other daughter are alive in Vietnam," he said.

Đường Bảy apologized and explained that he couldn't stand his daughter's suffering. Ba looked at him, eyes softening. "My children suffer too," he said. "We all suffer."

When we awoke on the third day with the sun overhead, we had no water left, and Má immediately began praying for rain. I remember looking at the cool water visible for as far as the eye could see, and I reached down, feeling the relief on my scorched hand. Then touching my wet hand to my lips, I suddenly realized why salt ruined any chance of real relief. My hand burned some, but my cracked lips were on fire. I felt as if I had put alcohol on my face after an afternoon training in martial arts.

Most of the time I stared at the ocean, always reminding myself that it was an illusion of relief—a lie. Without any water left, Ba and Má had us kids collect our own urine to drink. It was gross, but we had to try something or give in to eventual death.

That night, we again faced the waves. Rain sprinkled down from the sky, and Má took the tarp and made a funnel into a bucket to collect the fresh, liquid gold. But the saltwater kept splashing over the side of the boat, spoiling our fresh water. With the rain, the waves were worse; we could hardly keep upright, but the boat still held. At one point Ba said, "This is it. The boat is going to flip. This is it."

But Má swore at him, saying, "I will not give up. Not until my last breath," and she grabbed the long shaft of the trolling motor at the back of the boat and used the shaft to help keep the boat balanced. It worked—just enough to keep the boat upright through the night.

The fourth day when I woke up to the high sun, I realized that I was waist deep in water. I tasted the water we had saved from the rain, it burned my nose and throat. But it was all we had. Though Bác Hai could tell our general location, he really had no idea where we were anymore. Who knew where the waves had carried us.

That night wasn't as bad as the others, otherwise we might not have had the strength to survive. While most of us didn't care anymore, Má kept us going. The following night, a storm came in suddenly, giving us the precious rain that we so desperately needed. "Thank you!" cried Má.

But again the rain brought even worse waves. Our boat rocked higher and higher, again and again. My father held the trolling motor's shaft in the water, trying desperately to balance our boat. To this day I have no idea how we survived, but Má insists that she saw the image of a glorious lady leading us out of the storm.

After the storm ended, we languished in the boat. Despite the extra water from the rains, I knew that the little kids, especially An and our little cousins, wouldn't last much longer. The day shone hot and excruciating. But although we withered in the heat, we couldn't imagine facing another night of black, rolling waves. No food. No water. Just salt. That's all we had left: the breath in our lungs and the salt on our skin.

Maybe our prayers would keep being answered. Someone still continued watching for ships. I don't know if any of us actually thought we would see anything, so when Chú Bảy yelled, "Ship! It's a ship!" none of us heard him. Again he yelled about the ship, and within seconds, the boat that had been silent and still as the grave sprang to life. Ba and Bác Hai ran over to Chủ Bảy, looking out at the ship, while Má tied a white cloth to a stick and waved it in the air. We screamed and waved at the ship, "Over here! Over here!"

"Can you see the writing on it?" asked Ba. "Is it Thai?"

I knew what that meant—pirates. Straining my eyes to see the ship, I tried to make out the words. Could I read it? Was it the Vietcong? Which was worse?

We waited for the boat to come closer, excited and fearful. While we didn't want to die in this boat, there were some things worse than death.

In a few minutes we could make out the writing on the side of the boat; it was Thai.

CHAPTER SIX

BY THE TIME THE THAI ship got close enough for the men aboard to communicate with us, I was filled with dread. I could see men with bright white faces in tight shorts, the men's bare chests and arms dark from the sun. Mà asked Ba to yell at the men in English to see who they were and what they wanted. He complied; Ba and Bác Hai yelled at the ship to stop until it finally pulled alongside us. A man looked down at us over the side, his eyes flitting back and forth, taking in our situation. He yelled at his men, and his men threw down a rope ladder. Though Bác Hai said he would go first because he spoke the best English, Ba insisted on going with him. One after the other both men climbed up the rope ladder and disappeared over the side of the boat.

After a few minutes, Mà turned to Chủ Bảy and yelled at him to go help his brother, but when Chủ Bảy had climbed halfway up the ladder, Ba's head appeared over the side. "It's okay! They're fishermen. Climb up!" he said.

The fishermen lowered a large basket over the side and pulled the little kids up. The rest of us had to climb, and as soon as we were safely on board, Mà and Thiem Bảy praised Buddha.

A man, whom Ba explained was the captain, stepped forward. The captain sent the women and children into his cabin to rest. The fishermen brought us water, and we guzzled it as fast as we could, but a Thai man yelled at us and mimed sipping the water slowly. Ba told me later that it was dangerous for people as dehydrated as we were to drink so quickly—it would make us sick.

After a while, Bác Hai and Ba came over and took some water, sipping it slowly. Má leaned over and asked Ba what had happened when Ba and Bác Hai had first boarded the ship. He said that the Thai captain had asked why we were there, who we were, and how long we had been stranded in the ocean.

"Why are their faces so white?" I asked.

"It's powder. It protects their faces from the sun," said Ba.

I was about to ask why they didn't just wear more clothes, when some of the white-faced men came over, bringing with them platters of food, a feast—curry, fish, and fruit. After years of living off whatever our family could scrape together, I'm not sure I could have even imagined this much food. Even better than the food was the soda. After the war, I had never seen this treat.

Even in our starved state, we couldn't finish off all the food. Ba and Má made sure that my siblings and I didn't eat ourselves sick, but they too felt the relief of a full belly. After we had finished eating, the Thai captain came back over and told Ba and Bác Hai something in English. Ba and Bác Hai protested, pointing at the rest of us on the deck of the ship. But the captain kept shaking his head.

"What is he saying," I asked Má. "Do you know?"

"Má pursed her lips. "The captain has said that he won't be able to take us to shore," she said.

"Why not," I asked.

Má shushed me. "The little ones might hear," she said.

I sat there, stunned. After the captain left, I turned to Ba and asked, "Má says the captain won't take us to shore. Why not?"

Ba's face looked so tired, but he put on a brave face for us, like he always did. "He says that the Thai government is refusing to let in any new Vietnamese refugees. They didn't have enough resources to take care of them all. Like in my brother, Chủ Sâu's letters, remember? He told us that it was bad in Thailand."

"But can't he help *us*? We will die out here, Ba!" I said.

Ba shook his head again. "No," he said. "The Thai captain says that the government would confiscate his boat and imprison him if he tried to help us. Then we would be sent back to Vietnam."

"So he's just going to throw us back in the ocean and leave us to rot?"

"Hush. I told him that our motor wouldn't work, that we didn't have fuel or food, so the Thai captain is sending one of his mechanics to fix our motor. And he will send us off with fuel, food, and water enough to get us to shore." Ba paused, rubbing his head with his hand. "It's more than most men would do. Most Thai sailors would have just killed us."

As the sun began to set, one of the crewman handed a pair of binoculars to Ba and Bác Hai. When he was done looking through them, Ba turned and gave them to me. As I felt their weight in my hand, he said, "Look, there, across the ocean." Far in the distance I could see the rise of mountains and trees. Land! It was so close. "The crewman says we should see land by morning if we make good time in our boat," said Ba.

"They still won't take us to shore?" I asked.

"No," Ba said.

For half of that night, instead of facing the never-ending waves and bailing out water as fast as we could to save our lives, we rested on the boat, knowing we didn't have to worry about drowning or starving. We were safe—for now.

But around midnight, the Thai captain had us all get back in the boat, saying that he had taken us as close to the shore as he could. The entire time the crew prepared our boat to leave, Ba and Bác Hai begged the captain to change his mind, to take us into shore, drop us off anywhere. The kids were sobbing, and many of the adults were bowing to the captain, asking for mercy. One of the other sailors pulled the captain aside, gesturing at us and seeming to ask that the captain help us a little more. Eyes wet, the Thai captain kept shaking his head. He said he couldn't risk it. He had done too much already.

"Just one more hour. I'll take you in one more hour. I can't risk getting any closer to shore with Vietnamese refugees on my boat," he said.

When the captain decided that he had taken us as close to the shore as he could, he sent men into our boat to bail out the water remaining in the boat, leaving us the buckets. When the men had returned to the deck of the ship, we thanked the captain for the last time and climbed back down the ladder and back into the boat, which seemed even smaller than it did before. The men waved to us as they sailed away, the ship disappearing off the edge of the earth. Once the ship was gone, I noticed the size of the waves rocking our boat back and forth. But we had fuel this time. We could get to Thailand.

Ba started the motor, and we sailed through the night. In the dark I couldn't see the shore of the land ahead, but like the crewman had said, we should be able to see it by morning.

The next morning I woke up the sound of the motor; the sun rising over the water. Scrambling up to look over the side of the boat, I squinted in the direction we were heading. But I couldn't see anything. "Ba?" I said. "Do you see land?"

"No, Tuấn," said Ba. "None of us have seen it yet. But it's early; there's still time." Everyone in the boat silently ignored the alternative: that we might have gotten turned around in the night or that the Thai fisherman may have lied to us. I remembered the captain's shaking head and his refusing to help us. *Had he been that desperate to avoid arrest? But then why would he feed us and give us fuel if he planned to take us further out to sea?* I am sure I wasn't the only one puzzling through these worries, but the adults didn't appear agitated, their faces turned towards the direction of the unseen shore.

Two silent hours passed before the adults began whispering to each other in the back of the boat. I guessed they must finally be giving voice to the worries I had been thinking about since sunrise. Dejected, I went to the front of the boat, and sat down to stare out across the water. Wave after wave rolled beneath us. The sun continued to beat down, making me squint against the sparkle of the ocean. In the distance, at what looked to be the edge of the world, part of the ocean seemed dull, almost blurred against the horizon. The blur grew craggy and filled with trees.

"Ba!" I yelled. "Land!" At first, no one seemed to hear me, but I yelled over and over. "Land! Land!"

Ba yelled back, "What? Are you sure?" He ran up to the front of the boat, letting Chủ Bảy take the motor and squinted into the distance. "Yes, Tuấn. It is! It's land!"

Soon everyone was shouting and rejoicing for getting us this far. I imagined the feeling of the solid ground beneath my feet, a chance to leave the dark waves, heat, and dehydration behind. But after two hours, we didn't seem much closer to the shore.

"Ba!" I said. "Why is the shore still so far away? How long will it take to get there?"

"Oh," he said, "About five or six more hours."

"Ah!" I cried, 'So long?"

Ba laughed, actually laughed, and said, "You can see the land, but we still are miles and miles away. But we'll get there. We have the fuel." He was so pleased, so happy that we were about to land on shore, about to finally enter a new land, leaving behind the one that had become so hostile and foreign to us. His smile looked so strange on his face, like somewhere, between the war, imprisonment, and struggle for our very survival, he had lost his expression of joy and could no longer feel the sense of happiness. But here, despite our long journey, he had found it again; he had found his joy.

The hours dragged by as the small spot of land in the distance grew larger. I kept thinking, worrying that something would happen, that we would be picked up by pirates or that a storm would roll in, and we would never make it to land.

But by the end of the day, we were landing on the shore of a new world. As I stepped out of the boat into the shallow water of the shore, I felt the sand give way beneath me, making me unsteady on my feet. I fell to my knees and felt the gritty earth between my fingers and felt that our seven days at sea had taught me never to take dry ground for granted. I looked up at the land, half expecting to see the familiar expanse of water spread before my eye, but instead I was looking at a strange grouping of small buildings. It felt like I was one of the first explorers on Mars. The buildings near the shore were different colors and decorated with animal horns curving up at the corners of the roofs. And though we did have similar trees back in Vietnam, some of the other vegetation looked strange.

As the eighteen of us gathered on the beach, the people of the village came out of their houses, speaking to us in Thai. Bác Hai and Ba tried to speak to them in English, but neither party knew enough to communicate well. They managed to tell the villagers that we were Vietnamese refugees seeking asylum, but unlike the captain of the Thai ship, these people's faces didn't soften; they didn't offer us any food or water. But we didn't care. Against all odds, we had made it to land. The monstrous sea, the burning sun, nothing had stopped us from getting to this moment. We were free.

After about half an hour, we learned why the people were unwelcoming—the Thai military police were coming. Somehow the government had learned that we had landed. A jeep and a covered government military truck drove up, and an officer got out of the jeep, yelling at us in Thai. Ba and Bác Hai yelled back in English, Bác Hai stepping forward to translate.

"Is this all of you?" asked the officer.

"Yes, yes," said Ba. "This is all of us."

"We Thai have taken in many of you homeless Vietnamese, but we have no more room. So you have to go back, back to Vietnam."

Ba and Bác Hai tried to argue with the officer, but the officer shouted and waved his gun at us. The soldiers surrounded us, herding us into a circle on the beach.

The officer kept yelling at us, waving his gun at the boat. "Get back in the boat. You have to leave. Now."

"But we'll die!" said Ba.

"That's not my problem," said the officer.

We all got back in the boat, fearing that if we delayed any longer that they would shoot us. The little kids began to cry, clinging to Má and

Thiem Bảy. The soldiers then tied a rope to our boat, attaching it to a larger boat, and began to tow us back to the ocean. They towed us over a couple of hours before they cut the rope, shooting their M-16s into the air and yelling at us to go back where we came from, a place that they didn't realize no longer existed. Once again, we were here, surrounded by the monstrous waves of the ocean.

Everyone sat in shock and watched the Thai soldiers sail off back towards the shore. As the sun began to set, the waves rolled across the ocean, rocking our boat back and forth.

"Well," said Bác Hai, "What are we going to do now?"

Chủ Bảy said, "We have no fuel." He paused to think for a moment and then threw up his hands. "That's it. We just have to sink the boat and swim."

Everyone looked around at each other, at the waves, and at the children sitting in the adults' laps and in the bottom of the boat.

"You're right. I guess we will," said Ba. "We'll have to take that chance."

I thought, *He has to be kidding. Swim now? When we are this tired?*

"Wait," said Đường Bảy. "Swim? My daughter can't swim. The smaller kids can't swim. How are we supposed to get to shore?"

"We have a little fuel left, so we get as close to shore as we can; then, we swim," said Ba.

Đường Bảy ran his hand through his hair and readjusted himself in the boat. "But we *can't* swim that far. We'll all die," he said.

Ba looked around at everyone. "We will all die if we stay here. We can't spend another night bailing out the boat. There's no point, and we are too close not to try," he said. "We can do it."

Má said, "We will have to decide who watches over each of the children." She paused. "Each family should decide that for themselves."

As the waves grew larger, Má kept bailing the water out as it came, buying us time as Ba worked on the motor. Ba took the little gas that was left in the long-shafted trolling motor and put it in the main motor. After several tries the motor started, and we were on our way.

During the next hour or so, I kept thinking about the eighteen of us swimming to shore. How far was the shore? I couldn't see it in the distance at all. How far had the Thai soldiers taken us from the shore?

The motor suddenly stopped, sending us adrift in the ocean. Má looked back at Ba, who nodded his head. Má gathered the children and explained that we were going to get into the water. "Don't be afraid," she said. "Ba and I will take care of you."

Má and Thiem Bảy got into the water, and Ba and Chủ Bảy handed down the kids one at a time. The kids began screaming, kicking out their legs. "I don't want to go in the water!" they screamed. Ba and Chủ Bảy tried to reassure them as they grabbed each child and lowered him or her into the water.

I got into the water too, and Đường Bảy handed me his small daughter, Bến. "Hold onto her tight, Tuấn. Do not let her go for anything," said Đường Bảy. I nodded.

The men still in the boat began the process of sinking it to show no sign that we were ever here. I thought it strange that though we had spent night after night trying to save that boat, to keep it afloat, now we were sinking it. Our vessel of safety was finally sinking beneath the waves.

The adults, including Trường and me, had at least one child to look after. Turning on our backs, we floated on the water, letting the current carry us to shore. For what seemed like hours we floated, riding the incoming tide. Sometimes I would turn, checking to see if the shore was any closer, but I couldn't see it in the dark. As I lay there, staring up at the stars, I wondered if we would ever reach land again, if we would ever get back to shore, leaving this water behind.

I wondered at how I got here, floating in the ocean, far from my home country, not having any idea where I was. My mind flashed back through our journey, leaving the rest of our family back in Vietnam without even saying goodbye. I thought about the small bit of Thailand I had already seen, the colorful houses, the strangely decorated roofs. Would we live in a place like that? How would we start over again in a new country?

But I had made a new home once before. In 1975, the country that I called home ceased from existence, making my family and me instant foreigners, outcasts standing on land no longer our own. The Vietcong had done everything they could to destroy us, making sure we were always aware that our lives were not our own. Here in this moment, I decided that no matter how many times my family had to start over, we would. Má's fierce determination and Ba's silent persistence had gotten us this far. With my family, we could survive anything; I just knew it.

Though I felt like I was going nowhere, I knew I had to keep going, so I kicked out with my feet. But my right foot got stuck in the water. My head flew up and I shoved my foot farther down in the water, my feet seeking purchase in the soft sand. Suddenly I was standing waist-deep in the water, staring at the sandy beach. Walking forward, I set Bến down on the beach, and fell to my knees on the beach. No Thai soldiers were in sight; we weren't going back in the ocean.

I shouted, "We are in shallow water!"

The others repeated the phrase back to me, "We are in shallow water!" like the echo in a cave. Kids were dragged onto dry land by their parents or older siblings until all of us were accounted for and resting out of the water.

As I lay on the sand, I tried to get used to the solid ground under me. I just couldn't believe it, but it was true. We had made it to shore.

Hours later I woke up on the beach; the sand beneath my face felt cool and gritty, sticking to the moisture still left from the sea. At first it felt as if the ground was still moving beneath me, my face rubbing in the grit. Land. It must be. So I lifted my head to look around. Beach stretched down the coast, waves pulling out layers and layers of sand.

Around me, my family was gathered in little groups. After we had landed last night on the beach, we had made our way up the shore away from the water, finding a safe place to rest.

Suddenly, a loud roar shook the ground, sending us to our feet and making the children scream. The men yelled back and forth to each other, trying to figure out where it came from. Were we being attacked? Had the Thai soldiers found us?

But no, a train flew past us on tracks hidden behind vegetation. Má and Thiem Bảy wrapped their arms around the little kids, protecting them from the blasts of air and the noise from the train. After the train flew past, Ba and Chú Bảy looked at each other and laughed nervously. The rest of us smiled with relief. It wasn't explosions or guns or anything that we had been used to—it was the sound of civilization.

Now the morning sun crept over the horizon, illuminating the calming seas. But for the first time in days, we weren't looking at the rising sun from our decrepit boat. We saw it from the shore. I still couldn't believe I was alive, that the dark ocean hadn't swallowed me whole.

After several minutes, our little group gathered together, moving stiffly and slowly, exhausted and hungry. "We need to figure out what direction we are going to go," said Bác Hai.

I looked around the strange land on which we had washed up. As far as the eye could see, rows and rows of short plants grew in endless fields. Sparse trees sprouted here and there, except for the far horizon, where it seemed a line of trees grew at the edge of fields. Ba turned and looked where I was looking across the fields, then looked down the train tracks. "I think if we head down the tracks we may not reach civilization for days," Ba said. "So we should head towards those trees over there. Hopefully we'll run into a farmer or some other field worker who can tell us where the nearest village is."

Má and Thiem Bảy gathered the kids together, and we set off across the pineapple fields. I will always remember the rows of pineapple plants, like a spiky, pineapple desert. They seemed to mock my hunger and thirst, their thick skin deterring me from eating them. But Ba finally stopped and he and the other men began collecting the unripened fruit. The skin was so thick that the adults had to bite off the skin for the children before they could eat it. The acidity from the fibrous pineapple flesh stung our split lips and made our stomach queasy and unsettled. We walked away from the pile of pineapple skins more hungry and thirsty than before.

The pineapple juice dried into a sticky layer on my skin, continuing to warm and melt from the heat of the sun. I licked my sticky hand experimentally, but it didn't seem to help. When I looked up I saw something much better—a pond. Fresh water! It seemed that never before had such murky water tasted so sweet. I knew that the unclean water could be dangerous, but passing out from thirst would be much worse. We drank our fill, careful not to make ourselves sick, and ate more pineapple. With the water, the pineapple didn't feel so bad. I could already feel the sugar from the fruit give me some small, new strength.

As we all rested on the shore of the pond, I listened as the adults discussed our swim to shore the night before. Bác Hai couldn't believe that he had made it to shore with his leg cramping the way it did, and Thiem Bảy said in hushed tones that she almost dropped one of her children as she tried to keep the child's head above water. As I listened, I began to understand just how lucky we had been—we had all survived. Over in the group of adults, I heard Má echo my thoughts, insisting to the others that someone had been watching over us. She had been praying through the entire night, promising to give up meat for a month to please her god. Thiem Bảy nodded in agreement, saying she had been praying a similar prayer, and some of the men said they had promised to shave their heads if they made it through the night.

After we had rested, Ba stood and said that we should keep going and try to find a village somehow. The exhausted children cried while their mothers tried to soothe them. "We will be somewhere soon," said Má to Loan.

The sun, now directly overhead, beat down on our heads, with no cover or shade in sight. We didn't have any containers left, so we could not take any pond water with us. After walking another couple of hours, Ba had us stop to eat more pineapple, but it stung our mouths and again made us thirstier than before. Ba, insisting we press on, talked navigation with Bác Hai, both of them trying to estimate when we would find a village. My feet dragged, and my shirt stuck to my back with sweat. I began to hate the sight of pineapple, the symbol of the food I couldn't have. But suddenly, with almost no warning, we stumbled upon an old road, barely more than a dirt path.

"So there are people around here!" said Chủ Bảy, and Ba looked up the road and talked more with Bác Hai. Má praised Buddha for this sign, but when I looked up the road, it seemed to go forever. Faced with a visual of the distance we had yet to travel, my heart sunk into my chest. There was no way pineapple could get us that far.

I squinted again. A little ways down the road, I saw a tree I recognized. "A tamarind tree!" I shouted. "It might have fruit!"

In Vietnam, we used the tamarind's sweet fruit for sweet and sour soups, so I was familiar with its strange pods. They grew around the tree's canopy in clusters that would later remind me of skinny peanuts. The clusters would fall to the ground when they were ripe. We rushed to the tree and gathered the familiar fruit, lounging away from the heat afterwards. As I enjoyed the shade and something other than pineapple, I looked at the trunk of the tree and then up into the canopy of the higher branches. Looking up at the tree, I could almost pretend that I wasn't in Thailand. No pineapple. No ocean journey. Just a familiar tree back in Vietnam. I closed my eyes, enjoying my nostalgic illusion of safety.

But it was just that—an illusion.

CHAPTER SEVEN

ALL TOO SOON, BA SAID it was time to go. He was insistent that we needed to find some help before sundown if at all possible. We were about to head down the road again when a sound broke the silence. What was that? We had walked for miles all day and hadn't heard anything, but now we heard what sounded like a motor. I peered down the road and saw an old motorcycle with a sidecar.

As the motorcycle approached, I heard arguing among the adults about whether or not to flag down the motorcycle, but before anything could be decided, the motorcycle slowed and stopped in front of us. The man on the motorcycle and the man in the sidecar looked at us for a moment before speaking. The man on the motorcycle said something in English, and Bác Hai responded with what sounded like a question. The Thai man responded and then shook his head as he spoke. Bác Hai pleaded a bit with him, obviously asking for help, pointing at us. I could imagine how bedraggled we must look, skinny and gaunt, clothes stiff and unwashed. The Thai man spoke to the man in the passenger car, who got out and gestured at us to follow him. The motorcycle started up again and sped away down the road.

"What's going on?" Má asked Ba. Ba explained that the Thai men had immediately recognized us because their country has been flooded with so many Vietnamese, but their government has ordered them not to help us. "Then what is *he* doing?" Má asked, gesturing towards the Thai man up front who was walking with Bác Hai. Bác Hai must have heard because he turned back and said, "This man says he will take us to his house. The other man who drove away is his brother, who is going to make sure there is food and water ready for us when we arrive."

The entire group came alive with cheers of excitement and chatter. We would finally be able to eat. We just had to make it a little farther down the road. But after a while, the sun beat out most of our joy. The man's house must be terribly far for us to have walked this long. I leaned in looking for a breeze, like I had on the boat out at sea, but again, there was no breeze. Just heat. *At least*, I thought, *tonight we can sleep and not have to face the waves.*

Eventually I caught sight of the strange looking buildings on stilts, pillars maybe. A village in the air. As we got closer, we could smell the food cooking, and our spirits lifted, giving us new strength to walk faster. Our last good meal had been the night we spent on the fishermen's boat, and that had been days ago. As we came into the village, Thai people came out of their houses to look at us. We must have looked like a small army of ghosts, invading their peaceful village.

After introducing us to his family, the man pointed to the shade of the trees, and we sat down beneath a mango tree. The air was much cooler here, and we breathed more easily. I looked over at the man and his brother, their families standing around them, seeing kids not unlike my siblings and me. Did they think I must be similar to them too, or was it hard to imagine leaving their country for a foreign one? The brothers and their families brought us food and water, and we asked them to join us, but only the brother who had walked with us joined our meal. Like that night on the Thai ship, a feast lay before us—chicken curry, fish soup, and fruit. All familiar yet spicier with subtly different flavors. We ate an incredible amount, taking joy in being able to eat as much as we wanted. After we had eaten, the Thai man showed us a well out back where we could wash. Vietnam, being a country with almost as many waterways as roads, didn't really have wells. The idea seemed so strange to me: so much water in Vietnam compared to Thailand's dry earth.

Turning to Má, Ba said that he suspected something was going on.

"What do you mean? What's going on?" said Chủ Bảy.

"Some of the villagers have called the Thai police," said Ba. "They work with the government here."

"Will it be the same Thai policeman that took us back out to sea?" asked Đường Bảy. "If it is, we're all going to die."

Chủ Bảy swore, "What are we going to do now?"

"Pray. And we need to tell the kids something," said Ba.

Ba told us kids to rest while we could because the Thai brothers had said the Thai police would be here soon. But how could I really rest when all I could think about was the Thai men surrounding us, pointing their guns in our faces. The adults talked quietly, and I could guess their worries were about the Thai police officer. Would he send us back out in the boat again? I shuddered, thinking of the dark waves, rolling up and down, over and over. No, we couldn't go back to sea. We wouldn't make it this time. An adult asked why we had been fed if they were just going to kill us. Another responded that maybe it was one last kindness, a meal before we went to our death. I couldn't tell who said what; all the voices, all the worries began to blur and merge together. We prayed that the men coming wouldn't be the same as the ones who had sent us back out to sea. But they were.

When the military jeep and truck pulled up in front of the house, I saw it was the same officer that had sent us back out to sea. As the officer yelled at us and the Thai brothers, all the policemen got off the military truck, aiming their M-16s and hurrying to surround us. The officer walked up to our hosts' home and began to scream at them in Thai. It appeared from his body language that he was asking why they had helped us. He hit the brother that had escorted us to the house and pointed at us, continuing to scream at the top of his lungs.

He came over to us, yelling something. Ba later told me it was a lot of swearing and saying, "Where is your boat? We will find it and send you back to your own country!" Bác Hai tried to placate him and seemed to be begging the officer to help us. Later I learned that Bác Hai was saying that we had no country, no home to really call our own or to go back to. In the communists' eyes, we were no longer "real" Vietnamese. Bác Hai begged them to let us go somewhere, anywhere—even a refugee camp would be fine.

The officer yelled at Bác Hai, saying that their country and refugee camps were already overrun with Vietnamese. No more! At the time, I had no idea what he was saying, but I caught the word "Vietnamese" when he spat it out. At this, Bác Hai spoke again quickly, but this seemed to make the officer even angrier. The officer raised his gun at Bác Hai's head, and the soldiers followed suit, raising their guns at the rest of us. Má began to pray, but someone shouted at her to shut up. The kids sobbed in terror, and even some of the adults' faces were streaked with tears of fear. I heard one of the Thai brothers pleading with the officer, but he was shouted at, pushed, and quickly quieted. Suddenly, Thiem Bảy fainted, and Chủ Bảy began trying to hold up his wife. A Thai woman tried to run forward to help, but she was stopped by a soldier who aimed his gun at her. Má also saw Thiem Bay collapse in Chu Bay's arms so she ran forward, ignoring the yelling officer, and laid Thiem Bay down on the ground. Má then began massaging Thiem Bay's forehead with her own two knuckles, trying to make Thiem Bay regain consciousness.

I couldn't stop thinking about all of the effort we had gone through to escape the violence of Vietnam just to find a new, equally violent country here. When suddenly, the officer lowered his gun and gestured at the soldiers. Before I quite knew what was happening, we were herded into the military truck. As the truck pulled away, the Thai people waved sadly at us, seeming to know that whatever awaited us couldn't be good. We couldn't understand their language, but we could still tell they didn't want us to be taken away or treated so violently. The sun was sinking below the treeline, the darkness descending upon us with its silent calm.

Tears ran down our faces. We were terrified, not knowing where we were going. At least right now we didn't have to face the monster of the sea, of mother nature; but soon I caught sight of the tamarind tree, and I knew were going back the way we had come—back toward the ocean. The adults' whispers caught my attention; they thought the military policemen were taking us into the forest to execute us, but maybe, one argued, they were going to send us back to Vietnam. I didn't know which was worse. Soon I heard the waves, but we didn't stop. We kept driving for an hour or two, and I fell asleep, the exhaustion of the last weeks catching up with me.

When I woke up, I could see a dock, but to the left were houses, these same Thai houses with the decorative horns at the corners which seemed so strange to me. It was a town, at least compared to what we had been seeing. The truck came to a stop and the soldiers that had been riding in the back with us ushered us toward a Buddhist temple.

Oh, I could have wept with joy. They couldn't shoot us here; it was considered a sanctuary, a holy place.

The men barricaded us in the courtyard of the temple. After several minutes, Thai people from the town came to look at us, pointing, whispering, and laughing. My face grew hot, and I felt like an animal at the zoo. We all were able to sit down and rest, but that didn't stop the dozens of people coming to poke fun at us. Even today, far from Thailand and its people, whenever I go to the zoo, I think of that night behind the barricade and can't help feeling sorry for the caged animals.

After we had thought we were settled behind the barrier, soldiers grabbed Má and Thiem Bảy, and began to take them away. Ba and Chủ Bảy got up, begging the Thai men not to take them, but the soldiers ignored them and waved their guns at them. As the soldiers dragged Má and Thiem Bảy away, a monk appeared in the courtyard and grabbed Má and Thiem Bảy's hands, and spoke sternly to the officer. The officer, looking from the women back to the monk, slowly nodded and had the soldiers put Má and Thiem Bảy back behind the barricade. Satisfied with our confinement, he left, leaving behind only two soldiers to keep guard. Our families cried in relief and bowed to the monk and thanked him. He told us in English, "You're welcome," and then turned and spoke again to the guards. The guards nodded and the monk came over and gestured for us to follow him into the temple. In the temple, we lit incense in gratitude for getting this far.

Back in the courtyard, the Thai people who had come to gawk at us left one by one, and the Thai soldiers sat silently in chairs that they had found in the temple, always alert for possible escape attempts. There was no talk of escape, though. There was nowhere to go. A few hours later, the monk came back with some fruit and water that he first gave to the guards then brought over to us. We bowed again, thanking him for the food, which tasted wonderful. After we had eaten, we settled down with the blankets and pillows that the monk had also left for us. As the little kids fell asleep, the adults gathered, whispering in low tones. *What would happen now? What were the Thai soldiers going to do to us? At least it looked like they were going to keep us alive for now, but they still might send us back,* I thought. As I fell asleep I heard someone say, "But if they removed us from the temple? Wouldn't they shoot us then?"

Underneath the protection of the temple, we had the best sleep we had experienced since before we left Vietnam. But the next morning, the soldiers came back. The officer said something to Ba and Bác Hai in English, and the soldiers came forward and ushered all of the men into the military vehicles, taking them away without giving Ba or Bác Hai time to explain to the rest of us what was going on. As I watched the jeep take my father away from the safety of the temple, I remembered all of the times the Vietcong had come for my father, every new stint in the prison camps. Even here, in this strange new country, I had to wonder, would he come back this time?

Later that morning, the monks filed out of the temple and into the village, and I watched as they went door to door. At each house, a monk would offer up a bowl, and the villager would put some sort of vegetarian food in the dish, and the monk would give him or her a blessing, laying a hand upon the villager's head. After going through the town, the monks came back and shared their food with us, giving us fruit, rice, and tofu. The food was wonderful, but Ba's absence lay heavy on my mind. Má and Thiem Bảy tried to ask the monks where the soldiers took the men, but they could communicate only "work." So the men were out working? Was that right? Má and Thiem Bảy wondered if the soldiers were having them build a boat to send us back out to sea. No matter how much they speculated, they couldn't be sure.

All day I watched the world that sat beyond our little corner of the courtyard. Across from us I could see the beach. Mopeds, motorcycles, and the occasional car drove by. But my heart sank when I saw the Thai people coming back to look at us, chattering and pointing. Surprisingly some of the Thai people gave us food, and eventually, they straggled away, into the part of town I couldn't see. We waited for any sign of the military jeep and its officer to return with the men, but it was dusk when they finally returned. The men were herded back behind the barrier, and the monks brought us out food like they had the night before. Again no meat. *Má really is keeping her promise to give up meat that she made in her prayers,* I thought. *We all are.*

"Where did they take you?" asked Má. "What happened?"

"The pineapple fields. They had us working in the pineapple fields all day," Ba said.

The next morning the officer came and took the men out to work again. This time we didn't worry so much, but I still hated to see them go. After they left, I watched again as the monks went around collecting food. Later I saw monks carrying a bamboo boat coming down the road. This new culture fascinated me; the Thai people's respect for their holy men was so obvious. In Vietnam, we took food to the temple only on major holidays, and I wondered if the Thai people's respect for the monks explained why the soldiers listened to them so seriously.

That night the men came back and ate ravenously. They said they had been in the hot sun all day, working in the pineapple fields with just water and no food. The officer viewed them as dishonored refugees, former members of the South Vietnamese Army. Having now cheated death so often, both before and during our escape from Vietnam, even our current condition was a blessing.

After a week at the temple, we had fallen into a routine. The men left everyday, the monks collected food, and then we watched the road. But the day came when we didn't have to watch the road. Instead, our guards let us out to help the villagers. I learned that we were being kept in a fishing village because that was our primary task: unloading the boats of fish. But I didn't mind, and neither did the rest of us left at the temple. Most of the villagers were fair to us and paid us for our work, and we got out of the temple.

After a second week at the temple, the officer invited Ba and Bác Hai to have a drink with him back at his house. At first Ba and Bác Hai were suspicious, but it would have been a great insult to refuse such an honor. Besides, maybe they could convince the officer to send us to a refugee camp.

When they came back that evening from the officer's house, we surrounded them and asked them how the meeting had gone. Ba shrugged, "I guess we'll find out."

Over the next few days, the men started getting lunch at work, and the officer seemed to yell at them less and treated them with more respect. Finally, after hearing about this change in the officer's behavior, Má asked, "What did you two say to him?"

Ba explained that the officer had thought it was shameful for us to leave our own country, especially because Ba had been a member of the South Vietnamese Army. But Bác Hai had explained more about the war, about what had really happened. Outside of Vietnam, most of the world had received false information about the war. The South Vietnamese had lost not from lack of local support but from politics, propaganda, and lack of resources. Since the Paris Peace Accords in 1973, when the United

States began to withdraw from Vietnam, the South Vietnamese knew it was over. Without the support of the United States, the Vietcong would win the war.

Over 50,000[2] American and over 200,000[3] South Vietnamese soldiers died in the war. After the war, hundreds of thousands of civilians died at the hand of the Vietcong or the famine that followed the war.

One of the Vietcong's greatest strengths had been the charming lies they told about Vietnamese nationalism, public opinion, and the South Vietnamese. It wasn't only Vietnamese citizens who fell prey to these lies—the rest of the world often had too. "The North invaded the South," Bác Hai had told the officer. "We wanted to protect our country and our homes. And now, neither of them exist."

A few days later, the officer told Ba and Bác Hai that he was trying to get us into a refugee camp, but the Thai government was resisting. But he thought he could convince them. When Ba brought us this news, we rejoiced, so thankful that we could continue our journey to our new home. I could hardly believe the officer's change of heart. We had dreaded his coming so much, and now we looked for him everyday to see if he had any news.

We could wander about through the town on our own now, and I could go and catch some fish for a change. The vegetarian food the monks gave us was wonderful, but I missed fish.

We had been at the temple for a month when Ba brought word—the officer had said the government would have their final decision tomorrow. I cheered with the rest of them, and we all went in the temple to give thanks, the monks smiling with us and blessing us. None of us got much sleep that night, and the adults talked until morning. *Would we leave for the camp tomorrow? What if the Thai government refused to let us into a refugee camp?* Trying to ignore my mixed feelings, I slept fitfully.

The next morning we waited, but the officer didn't come at his usual early hour of the morning. We had to wait through the long morning hours before catching sight of the jeep pulling up. Our group surrounded him and peppered him with questions. He managed to get something out, and I knew it was a "yes" from the look on his face. We were already cheering by the time Ba and Bác Hai had a chance to translate. The officer said something to Ba, nodded and smiled, and then got in his jeep and drove away. "He says that we have to be ready tomorrow morning at five. It's a long drive to the camp."

The monks must have heard the news because they too were smiling, some with tears in their eyes. These kind men had protected and cared for us, perfect strangers, for what had seemed like such a long time. They were happy for us, but sad to see us go.

We had very little to gather that night, just a few things we had been given over the last month, mostly new sets of clothes. And that night we got less sleep than the night before because in the morning, we would leave for the next step in our journey.

CHAPTER EIGHT

THE TRIP TO THE REFUGEE camp took most of the day. At five in the morning we climbed into the same military vehicle that had picked us up and brought us to the temple, but at least this time, we knew where the Thai men were taking us. I had mixed feelings as we drove out of the village and waved back at the monks wishing us farewell. The truck drove down the road that had brought us into the village, passing through the rows and rows of pineapples. I watched the countryside until I saw the area where we had landed. The dark waves crashed against the shore beyond the train tracks. Had it really been a month already? I wondered if the Thai officials had ever found our boat. If they found it, would they make us repair it? When I asked Bác Hai, Chủ Bảy cut in and said, "You'd think they would send us back if they found our boat?"

"Don't say crazy things like that," said Bác Hai.

"He always says stupid things," said Ba, laughing and giving Chủ Bảy's arms a shove.

Around 1:00 in the afternoon we reached Bangkok, and the truck stopped briefly to pick up some food before hurrying on. The Thai soldiers with us explained that we still had several hours to go. Soon we headed into the mountains towards the city of Nakhon Ratchisma. It seemed like our truck wound around the mountain roads forever, my body baking in the sun and the movement of the vehicle making me sick to my stomach. I wondered if they were taking us to the edge of the earth. Several times the truck looked like it was heading off the road and down the side of the mountain.

"I hope they don't take us up in the jungle to live with the monkeys," said Ba.

"Are you sure they're going to take us to the refugee camp?" asked Chủ Bảy.

"Just wait a little longer," said Bác Hai, his face betraying his anxiety.

Ma and Thiem Bảy began to discuss the situation in worried tones. Was the camp really up these mountains? Why would they put a camp at the end of such a dangerous road? Ba and Chủ Bảy tried to keep their wives calm, reassuring them that the truck has to travel slowly because of the roads, and there was no reason to worry.

Finally, we stopped at a gate before a large compound. On a sign near the gate, Vietnamese script said, "Sikhiu Refugee Camp." We had made it. Someone said something in Vietnamese on the loudspeaker as the gate opened and the truck drove through and stopped at the second gate. I looked around, taking it all in. Barbed wire ran at the top of the walls the entire way around the perimeter of the compound. I remember being a bit surprised at how secure the camp was.

Family photo at Refugee camp in Sikhiu

The camp guards opened the second gate, and we drove through and were met by a crowd of people shouting at us in Vietnamese. From what they were saying, they were looking to see if they knew us. I felt shocked at hearing Vietnamese after a month of hearing only Thai spoken. I could understand what people were saying!

After we stopped at the front office, an official came out and told Ba and the other men in our group to sign some papers, while the rest of us stayed in the truck and watched the refugees milling in the yard. When Ba and Bác Hai came out, they told us that we were all placed in the same building. Soon, a man came up to us and introduced himself as Quan, the leader of our building, Building 12.

First we headed to a warehouse where each person was given a blanket and pillow, and each family received a five-gallon bucket, a bag of rice, an allotment of fish, and some clothing. Quan lead the way to our building, explaining how things work at Sikhiu. He said that the camp was about five square miles and held about 5,000[4] Vietnamese refugees. I learned that the camp had three housing zones—A, B, and C—with zones A and B being the oldest and most spacious. Zone C was added later when the camp needed more space for refugees. Every person had to be in his or her zone at the 10:00 nightly curfew, or be put in prison.

"So this is like prison?" said Ba.

"You could say that," said Quan.

I paused, trying to take it all in while my mind raced with confusion. *Curfew? Prison?*

As we passed different parts of the camp, Quan would point them out. The Buddhist temple and the Lutheran, Baptist, and Catholic churches sat in one section of the camp near an open area. There was a school where the younger kids went in the morning and the older grades went in the afternoon. We passed a market, a cafe, and food stalls. Each reminded me, in a way, of Vietnam.

When we got to Building 12 in Zone C, we were shown to our own section of a large open building. Other families had already sectioned off their parts of the building, creating a sea of blanketed, temporary walls. The building had lights on the ceiling and a metal roof but no air conditioning or fans, so the building emanated heat. Beds lined the side walls of the building like benches attached to the wall. Each family was assigned about three feet of bed, which was a little wider than a foot, for each person in the family. After we dropped off our things, Quan led the way out back to the building's water tank. Each family used their five gallon bucket to get their water, which ran from the tanks twice a day—for just fifteen minutes each time. The bigger your family, the more water you were allotted. Quan explained that when the alarm went off, you had to have someone get in line to get water or you wouldn't get any. At this elevation, the camp's only access to water came from streams and small rivers. In a country that was this hot, water was gold.

Quan explained that every family was assigned a day where they were in charge of keeping the outside of the building spotless. Everyone sixteen and older had to help; if your family failed, then those in charge of cleaning that day would be put in jail. Finally, Quan emphasized his last point: we had to go line up for the Thai national anthem twice a day. You had to be seriously ill, *very* seriously ill, to miss lining up for the anthem. If you missed the anthem, if your children weren't behaving, or if you fell over from heat stroke, you would be put in prison or hung by your wrists at the front gate of the camp. Worse, this offense would go in your permanent file, so countries interviewing you to possibly take you into their country would see that offense.

My mind whirled with this information, my previous joy at arriving at Sikhiu evaporating in the heat of Building C. But throughout the next days, I realized that Quan's introduction to camp life represented a much longer and painful initiation. In the following days, we learned more about the immigration process, how people went months, sometimes years without getting out. Horror stories of the "interviews" required to qualify to move to another country deflated our hope even further. Ba and Má began rehearsing their answer about Ba's work with the American military, each memorizing the exact set of dates and military information. Thankfully, Má had managed to carry over paperwork from before the end of the war, ensuring that they had proof of father's loyalty to the United States and membership in the South Vietnamese Army. She had guarded this paper work for years, knowing that, one day, our American IDs could ensure our freedom.

The second day at camp, we had to register at the main office to get on the list for an interview with immigration services. My father's brother, Chủ Sâu, had sent us a letter instructing Ba that he should drop his children's ages so that we would have some time to learn the language and to catch up in school. Ba listened to his brother and dropped each of our ages by two years. According to Immigration Office, and all official documents to this day, I had been born in 1971 instead of 1969.

In the camp, we soon learned that former communist informants had also fled Vietnam after realizing the Vietcong were cruel dictators rather than the saviors they had imagined, so they were in the camp with us. Because the United Nations frowned upon communist supporters, some of them stayed in the camp for over five years. At first I was furious when I learned that Vietcong supporters were in the camp. We lost everything because of them. But Ba explained that the Vietcong had forced many of these families to join the communist party by threatening the villagers' families. So despite everything these former communists had supported,

I began to feel more sympathy for them as I learned more and more about the camp.

Each family had a limited amount of food, and the perishable items were often spoiled or rotting. Without Chủ Sâu sending us money, I am not sure how we would have made it. Even so, Chủ Sâu was struggling himself and would sometimes forget to send us money. Ba discovered that we could write to international sponsors that might send us money. We sent out hundreds of letters. Though we gained two sponsors, it still wasn't enough for a family of seven. So Má rolled up her sleeves and did what she did best—she found a business to earn us extra money.

Every morning, Má set up a food stand and began selling Vietnamese omelettes. Very quickly she gathered popularity and a set of regulars. In

Trường, Loan, Phong, and a friend

addition, my brothers and I would get up at five every morning and get banh mi, a type of bread, for breakfast. We would dip the Banh mi in sweetened condensed milk and enjoy the warm delicious bread. After we had eaten, we took bamboo baskets around, hawking our wares, shouting, "Hot banh mi! Banh mi for sale!" We were able to keep ten cents of each baguette we sold, and soon we gathered sets of regulars who gave us a fairly steady income. Má gifted her entrepreneurial spirit to her sons, and it would stay with us the rest of our lives.

Our life in the camp reminded me of our life in Vietnam where everything was regulated and the threat of prison hung over our heads. But we had survived Vietnam; we could survive here. There was one big difference: we held hope for a brighter future here, one step closer to

America. I could see small glimpses of hope scattered across the camp, like in the special events held in the camp.

The leaders of the camp came up with the idea that if each building held back a certain percentage of rice every month or so, the guards would trade it to get an outdoor video projector. These movie nights were like camp holidays, with people reserving seats in the open field hours in advance. We watched U.S. westerns, Chinese movies, Thai movies, and I loved every one.

Tuần at the New Year

The camp also had a soccer team that would often play a local Thai team. These games drew people from all over the camp, and created large crowds around an open grass area near the churches. But after every movie day or soccer game, camp residents had to return to reality—lining

Trường with friend at the outdoor cinema

up for the Thai national anthem every morning and evening. One time, a man cut in front of Chủ Bảy in the water line, and Chủ Bảy refused to let it go, saying he was there first. The result ended in a fist fight that landed both men in prison. Worse, Chủ Bảy was hung in front of the camp. Under the scorching Thai sun, Chủ Bảy hung for almost two days. The sun scorched his body, his skin blistering in the heat, and I worried he would die from dehydration. There happened to be a soccer game that first day, so I walked back in forth with the crowds, carrying water and making sure that I "tripped" and spilled water over my uncle, sometimes even stopping long enough to pour water into his mouth. People crowded around me, hiding my efforts. If the guards noticed that I was trying to help, I would be arrested, hung up right beside Chủ Bảy. Eventually Chủ Bảy was let go, but the damage was done: we knew that this would go on his family's permanent record.

The threat of an offense on our permanent records suddenly became more real. It could really happen. I remember a particular instance when I became really sick with vomiting and fever. I became dehydrated and dizzy, Ba had to help me outside to line up for the national anthem. Right before the anthem started, my strength failed, and I fell into the dirt. A guard came over, yelling that if I didn't stand on my own for the entire duration of the anthem, I would be put in prison. Ba said no, that if I fell, *he* would go to prison in my place. My heart sank at the thought of Ba hanging in the front of the camp—like Chủ Bảy—and that offense, *my* offense, going on our permanent record.

So, digging deep, I stood, trying to avoid the Thai guard's dark eyes, which watched me, waiting for me to fall. Somehow, I managed to stand through the entire song. As soon as the anthem ended, I fell into my father's arms, and he helped me to our compartment. I made it. I had won.

Má, Ba, and Chủ Thiem Bay at Sikhiu Camp

Ba and Má worried about us in the refugee camp almost as much as they worried about family still back home. Now that we were in a place that was stable enough for us to send letters, Má and Ba wrote to our families back in Vietnam. Crafting a letter to someone in a communist country is an art. Nothing suspicious or negative could be included, but the letter still needed to find a way to tell our families that we had made it to the refugee camp and we had survived. After sending their letters, Ba and Má waited anxiously for a response. Every day before lining up for the Thai national anthem, they would wait anxiously for their names to be yelled in mail call. After a few months, letters finally began to arrive.

Ba learned that his youngest brother, Chủ Út, had been arrested by the Vietcong for helping us, and Chủ Út's possessions and land had been seized, forcing his wife and children to move back in with his wife's parents. It would be years before Chủ Út was released, and when he got out, his arm was paralyzed from the torture and mistreatment he had endured from the Vietcong.

When Má eventually heard from her mother, she learned that her two brothers had gone into hiding after being accused of helping us escape. But they hadn't even known of our plans, let alone helped us. Má was devastated, and she cried for days. She wrote back asking for more news, and when a reply came, she learned that her mother had been put in prison until her brothers had turned themselves in. Bà Ngoại had tried to talk to her brother, my mother's uncle, who was high up in the communist party, to free her sons. But her brother had refused.

Bad news after bad news came in these letters, but Má still waited anxiously for every one. I began to realize how much our entire family would suffer because of our escape. I felt that I would never be entirely free from this feeling of guilt.

As we fell into our way of life at Sikhiu, I began to make friends with the other kids at my school. We shared our survival stories, assuring others that we had the best survival story. Though I initially tried to one-up the other kids with my story of horrible nights at sea, lack of food and water, and violent Thai soldiers, I soon realized that my family had been blessed beyond comprehension.

I heard of girl who had been escaping with her family and a couple hundred others on a large boat, making the same journey my family had made from Vietnam to Thailand. At some point on their way across the ocean, Thai pirates captured the girl's boat. The pirates raped the women and teenage girls, killing any men who tried to rescue them. The women were thrown back in the boat and sent adrift, forced to suffer the same fate if any other pirates came by. At some point, the girl's boat was hit by another boat, throwing the girl into the water. The girl floated on debris for a long time, so long that the skin on the half of her body in the water became loose and wrinkled. Fish began to nibble at the edges of her body until she was rescued and brought to Sikhiu to live in the orphanage there.

I saw this girl around school, and I tried not to stare at her skin, which still looked severely burned in the places that had been soaked in the water. I heard story after story, each one worse than the last.

But none was worse than that of my friend. I sat by Trung at school, we became friends, and soon he began coming home with me. It wasn't long until I heard Trung's story.

Trung and his family fled Vietnam in a large boat that held about four hundred people, each person cramped into an incredibly small space. Several boats of pirates overtook them, tying up the men and younger children. The pirates raped the women—mothers, wives, daughters—taunting those tied to try to help them. After the pirates finished with the women, they threw each woman overboard. Tied and helpless, Trung could only listen to his mother's and sisters' screams until they faded beneath the waves.

The pirates showed no mercy, killing each captive man, including Trung's father and brothers.. Trung told me that he was sure this was it. He was going to die. He had watched as the pirates got closer to where he was tied, but for some reason, the pirates stopped, deciding to leave a handful of young boys. The pirates sailed away, showing no sign of remorse for the devastation they had caused.

Trung, wondering how he would untie himself, tried to roll around, but suddenly, a few small children crawled from the corner of the boat and began to untie those left behind. For days, the children on the boat drifted across the ocean. No food. No water. They had been left in the ocean to die. Trung said that at some point he had passed out and later woke up in a German humanitarian rescue boat, which had eventually brought him to Sikhiu. But his family was dead. He was alone with hundreds of other parentless children.

I told my parents Trung's story, and although I am sure they had heard many like it, they held a special place in their hearts for Trung. Trung began calling my parents *Má* and *Ba* as well, and they called him *son*. He spent his free time with us, and when we could, we tried to fill the emptiness in his heart.

Not all of my friends brought such sadness. I met a girl, Hiên. At such a young age, we had an innocent relationship of young love, meeting to stand around awkwardly and talk. But I had never felt this way before, and this first girlfriend reassured me that life, despite being confined to a refugee camp, could have some semblance of normalcy. Impossible as it may seem for all the horror, people grow up. Life goes on.

After a year at Sikhiu, the day came when we heard our name called over the loudspeaker. The next day we would have our interview. Ba had become angry at Chủ Sâu for sending money to Chủ Bảy but not to us. When his family had needed him most, Chủ Sâu had turned his back on his oldest brother. Chủ Sâu hadn't helped us like a family member should, which was, in Vietnamese culture, one of the greatest dishonors. Ba insisted that he no longer wanted to go to America; he wanted to go to France where our sponsors were, so when he discovered the interview was with the American government, Ba refused to go.

The evening before the interview, Má begged him to go. Pleading and cajoling soon turned to yelling, Má insisting that they had not come this far to give up because of a petty family dispute. "America is a big country," she said. "You don't even have to see him if we go."

But Ba refused. The morning of the interview, Má got ready and

Má and Ba's Photo IDs

begged Ba to do the same. Even our neighbors told him he was an idiot if he didn't go. He had worked for the Americans. He was sure to get in. Somehow, their combined efforts changed his mind, and he begrudgingly agreed to go.

The immigration officials separated my parents, aggressively questioning them separately. Then the immigration officer called me in, asking me about my parents' story and making me feel interrogated. But because Ba's documentation proved that he had worked with the American GIs, the Americans approved our family to immigrate to the United States. Má and the rest of us hugged each other, thrilled that our journey might come to an end. But Ba angrily asked the immigration officers from America if he could go to France instead. They said no, and then they informed him that if he didn't go to America, it would be on his permanent record and other countries would be less likely to accept us into their country. Ba finally agreed to go to America. Chủ Bảy, despite his run-in with the Thai guards, had also been in this round of interviews, and so had Đường Bảy and his daughter Bến. Though we worried that Chủ Bảy's record might work against him, he and his family had also been approved to immigrate to America.

We had a week before we were scheduled to leave, so we spent that time celebrating with the friends we had made in the camp, especially my girlfriend, Hiên. We both knew that we would likely never see each other again. I tried to reassure her that I would write her, but we knew it would never be the same. And Trung, now family in everything but name, could not come with us. These dear friends, the best of my life at Sikhiu, had to stay behind.

When it was time to leave, my family piled into one of two large buses that had arrived to take us to Phanat Nikhom, the transitional camp. The trip lasted only an hour, but it felt like they had taken us to a whole new world. Phanat Nikhom, despite being a similar refugee camp, did not have the large fences to enclose its residents. At first this new freedom felt liberating, but we soon learned how dangerous this was for us. During the month we were there, our neighbor's daughter was abducted and held for ransom, but the humanitarian organization moving that family to

America did not have the money to get the girl back. By the time my family and I left, the girl still had not been returned.

To protect us from possible kidnappers, Ba kept watch through the night. During the day, we had to undergo tests and immunizations, preparing us for our move to America. But the camp barely gave us any food, and we had to save our money for our journey, so Má would buy fish bones to make broth for rice. Of course it was never enough, but I told myself that we would leave soon. Every moment at Phanat Nikhom kept me on edge, always preparing for someone invading our small apartment. Gangs would come by, assuring us that if we paid them, they would protect us, but my parents had heard that if we paid one gang, another would come and ask for money too.

I can't imagine living there any longer than we did. Fear embodies every impression I have of that camp—fear of not getting to America, of violence, of starvation, of death. It was Vietnam all over again.

CHAPTER NINE

WE PULLED AWAY FROM PHANAT Nikhom, and my chest filled with relief. As the bus drove through the mountains, I looked out my window and found myself looking down the side of the mountain. Terror dropped my heart into my gut, giving me the impulse to vomit as we wound our way up the road.

Always something else, one thing after another, I thought.

For several hours, we wound our way back and forth through the mountains to Bangkok. The movement caused several of the passengers to succumb to nausea, and the sweltering compartment become thick with the scent of sweat and vomit. By the time we reached Bangkok, the smell seemed to permeate our clothes, our possessions. Everyone's face bore the shocked expressions of being somewhat startled to be standing, alive and on solid ground. Because our plane would not leave until the next morning, we were ushered into a slightly run-down shelter, sort of like a hostel, and were told we would be sleeping here for the night.

Once the group from the bus was settled inside, the servers in the hostel gave us bowls of rice puree and wished us luck in our next life. I looked into my bowl, realizing this was the same rice dish that was said to prepare you for the next life. By eating the rice, you gave up your memories of your old life so you could start your new life with a clean slate, unaware of the horrors or joys you may have experienced before. The implications were clear: we had to let our past lives go, leave Vietnam behind, and embrace our new lives. *But how could I leave behind my country, my heritage?*

The years since we had lived in Cần Thơ had passed in a slow succession of loss. The market, my school, our little house next to Ông Nội and Bà Nội—all of it had disappeared so quickly. I looked up and saw the little kids shoveling in their food, unafraid of what would happen next, while my parents eyed their food wearily. As he looked at his food, Ba's face looked so much older than it had in Cần Thơ. Years in and out of prison camps had stripped away what had been left of his youth. The war—the nightmare that had robbed us of everything familiar including our way of life and our home.

I wasn't leaving behind my life today; the Vietcong took it away from me ten years before. I hoped our new life in America would give us more than what this bowl of rice porridge represented. Looking at my parents as they began to eat their food, I slowly lifted my bowl to my lips.

_____

The next day we got back on the bus and made the short trip to the airport. Everyone got off, and we were led through the front doors and up to the ticket counter. Around us, hundreds of travelers rushed around, heading in every direction. An immigration official gave us our tickets and led us through the airport, explaining that we were going to get food while we waited. As we walked, I stared at the huge building, and I noticed a strange room that people were entering. Doors would slide together, closing off the room, and when the room reopened, the people were gone. I asked Ba what the little room was, but he didn't know.

At the time, the most sophisticated city I had experienced was Cần Thơ before the war. In the ten years since then, I had been in a rural village as Vietnam closed its borders and time stood still. Very little new technology entered the cities of Vietnam, let alone the outlying villages. But the world around Vietnam had kept going, civilizations progressing and developing, implementing new technology and making new discoveries. Now I was seeing a small bit of what I had been missing. Electronic departure and arrival boards, fast food, and large jets. Even Ba said he hadn't seen this technology before and agreed this felt stranger than when we had landed on the shores of Thailand.

After several hours of sitting in the waiting area of our terminal, we boarded our plane, which felt to me like a small house. *How can something this big get off the ground?* I wondered in amazement. We buckled in and watched as the flight attendant gestured around the compartment—then the plane took off. It was like we were rocketing into space. I am not sure how long we were on the plane, but the sun was rising as we landed in Manila, Philippines.

Another immigration worker met us as we came off the plane and led us to a bus outside the airport. I paused before getting on, wondering if the bus would crash this time. But I took a deep breath and got on the vehicle with the rest of my family. By mid-afternoon, we were pulling into Bataan, the Philippines Refugee Processing Center (PRPC). I wasn't sure what to expect. Something like Sikhiu with tall, barbed wire fences? Or maybe the open arrangement of Phanat Nikhom? But the camp at Bataan was totally different. Arranged in an open format, Bataan looked less like a prison and more like a small town.

Once again we found ourselves checking into another camp, filing our paperwork, and receiving our housing assignments. PRPC had eleven zones, which included housing zones for the volunteer aid workers from around the world and zones for Laotians, Cambodians, Chinese, and, the largest group, Vietnamese.

While in Sikhiu we had been merely refugees. After we had been approved by the U.S. immigration officials, we were considered U.S. residents. Our new status gave us a freedom we hadn't experienced before Bataan. We could wander the zones as we pleased, take taxis or buses, and wander beyond the camp's boundaries into the jungle.

The officials told us that our family would stay in the PRPC for six months while we received additional medical attention, English language classes, and American culture and history classes. Each zone had its own adult English class, and my parents attended one of its two sections after being tested to see how much English they already knew. In addition to English as a Second Language (ESL) classes, the PRPC offered vocational and cultural training to help prepare us for our new lives in America.

Going to school in PRPC

Although there were several adult English classes, my siblings and I had to travel to the camp's only school, which was five zones away. I had never seen such a nice school building; I was used to schools that were barely more than bamboo or cement constructions, crowded, and dirty. My new teachers told me that the school was made to look like the schools in the United States to help get us used to what it was going to be like in America. But we still had school for only half a day, the younger grades in the morning and the older grades in the afternoon. I started school and quickly learned that most of the teachers were American volunteers.

One of the volunteers, a guy named John, told us about his home in America, a place called "The Bronx." At the time, I barely even knew the shape of the United States, let alone that John was from New York City.

But he was so proud of where he came from, I knew it must be a pretty great place.

John taught us about American football, played basketball with us, and—most memorably—took us on our first trip to McDonald's. When I first saw McDonald's, the restaurant looked unlike anything I had ever seen. After John ordered burgers and fries for us, we sat down in what John said was a "booth," telling us that this meal was the epitome of American cuisine. "It doesn't get better than this!" said John.

Cautiously I took a bite. The food tasted so strange—soft and fluffy. My family rarely had meat, let alone beef. As we ate, my friends and I talked among ourselves.

"This is the best of American food?" said Trang.

"I guess," I said.

"Then imagine how bad the rest of it is!"

We laughed, John looking at us with amusement, though he didn't understand what we said. He was used to us chattering away in Vietnamese. Though we teased about our strange meal, we thought the food was exotic and interesting, never having had food so different from our own.

But school wasn't all basketball games and new foods; I also had incredible amounts of homework. One morning I went to the library, trying to escape our small apartment for a chance to study. But no matter how much I tried to understand, my assignments still frustrated me. I banged

At the library

my fist on the library table.

"Excuse me, young man, do you need some help?" said a voice behind me. I turned around to a see a woman who looked to be about the same age as Bà Nội.

"What?" I asked. While I had learned more English, I could only understand the gist of what she said.

"Do you need help with your homework?" she asked again, gesturing at the paper and books on my table. Finally understanding, I nodded.

"I'm Miss Beverly," she said. "Let's see what you're working on, shall we?"

Miss Beverly helped me with my homework, using hand gestures and words I already knew to try to help me understand American geography, history, and culture. I came back the next morning and the next, and I doubt I would have had made as much progress as I did without her help. She had become a great friend. Soon Miss Beverly brought by potato chips or sandwiches for me to eat before school. These new foods seemed as exotic as the meal I had eaten at McDonald's with John and my friends. I couldn't help but wonder, what other foods like this would there be in America?

But I had months before I would find that out, so I tried to settle down in our temporary home along with the rest of my family. A month or two after we arrived, the head of security in our zone came to Ba and told him that he was leaving for America. Since his position would soon be available, he asked Ba to become the new head of security for Zone 5. Ba agreed and began patrolling the zone with about five other men, taking turns to keep watch at night.

On a few occasions, Ba would catch a Filipino man trying to break into one of the refugee's houses, the criminal often carrying a knife or some other weapon. Thankfully Ba's military training had prepared him to deal with robbers. But since Ba was just camp security, each time Ba caught one of these men he had to call the Filipino police to come take the captive away.

While Ba kept busy working security, Má created her own business, buying and selling the belongings of other refugees, making a decent living

Ba and Má on a night out

in the process. I know I shouldn't have been surprised, but Má's resourcefulness never ceased to amaze me. Sometimes she would take Trường and me up the side of the hill to cut down bamboo shoots to sell in the market, but more seasoned camp residents warned us to be wary of wandering too far into the jungle—rebels lived on the mountainside. When we were with her, Má made sure we didn't go too far, but it seemed like an adventure to me.

Of course, in my free time, I managed to find new friends with which to explore. Every evening we could, my friends, Mam and Trang, and I would walk around the camp and make our way to the river that served as the social gathering place for us refugees. Because we had no air conditioning or fans, the river provided the only relief from the heat and acted as our primary recreational center.

Back Row: Chu bay, Ba, Má, and Duong Bay
Front Row: My Den, An, Bich, Loan, and Ben

One day, we came up with a plan: we would go to the river in disguise every Sunday. Covering ourselves with mud, we dressed in Filipino clothing and headed down to the river, pretending we couldn't understand the whispers and insults thrown at us from the refugees. To make more trouble, we tossed rocks and other debris in the water to make the people even angrier, garnering more insults from the Vietnamese. Eventually we would startle them, shouting back in Vietnamese, often making them angrier. Sometimes we would climb trees and throw fruit at people below. One time an older woman began swearing at us at the top of her lungs.

Finally, Mam said, "Ma'am, why are you shouting at us? We're not Filipino; we're Vietnamese!"

The woman yelled at us even more, now cursing our parents for their lack of parenting skills. She finally walked away in a huff, and we burst out laughing. We never tired of this game.

No matter the circumstances, I always found trouble—at least that's what Má said. She may very well have been right. When my friends and I got bored of tricking the other Vietnamese, we decided to explore our temporary home—especially the mountainside. Time after time, we wandered into the jungle, cutting bamboo shoots, climbing the trees, and eating whatever fruit we found. Although we tried to be careful, we pushed our luck farther and farther. But one day we went too far.

One day after wandering through the jungle for several hours, we suddenly heard a sound. Turning around, we saw a few Filipino men through the trees. They were carrying guns.

Rebels! I thought, turning to run with Mam and Trang. But there were more men than we had thought, and they soon surrounded us, waving their guns. One of the men said something to us in what I could only assume was some sort of Filipino language, but I shook my head, sputtering in English. They saw our Filipino clothes we wore and thought we were Filipino.

"No! We're kids! Mean no harm! Vietnamese refugees!" One of the men stepped forward, and I repeated myself, adding "Sorry! Never again!"

The man said something to the others that I couldn't understand, then turning to us, he said, "Go! Never return to our village. Leave!"

We didn't have to be told twice. Running down the hill, I kept repeating to myself, "Never again! Never again!"

The camp officials had told us that we should be in PRPC for only six months, and Chủ Sâu sent us a letter, saying that he was trying to get a Lutheran church he knew to sponsor Chủ Bảy's family and our family to Minnesota where he lived. As our six months drew to a close, we knew we could leave at any time. I told Miss Beverly that my family would probably be moving to Minnesota, and she shivered.

"It's so cold there!" she said and pulled out a map of the United States, showing me where Minnesota was on the map. But each of the states seemed similar to me, and as one who had never experienced cold, I didn't really understand.

Our last day in the refugee camp

Families who had received sponsors and passed their medical examinations had their names put on a notice board, letting them know their departure date. My family began checking the board every day. Day after day we checked until, finally, there it was—our names. We were leaving. My entire family rejoiced; we were going to freedom and liberty in America! No more camps awaited us, just our new home.

Again I had to tell my friends goodbye, but for some reason, when I went to tell Miss Beverly we were leaving, I couldn't. Every time I thought of her kindly, grandmotherly face, my heart sank and I couldn't do it. When she asked when we were leaving, I could only say, "Soon."

When the day came that we had to leave, my family and I gathered with other families at the bus station long before our scheduled 6:00 a.m.

departure time. When the bus pulled up, I found my assigned seat with the rest of the family and stared out the window. This was it, the last leg of our journey.

A few hours down the road, we took a break at a rest stop to give us a chance to stretch our legs and take a breath of fresh air. I felt such an incredible sense of relief to get off that bus.The driver said he had received a call from the camp and we had to wait for someone, so we could take our time. The other passengers whispered among themselves, wondering who could forget that today was the day we were going to America?

About half an hour later, we saw a car coming down the road toward us, and I shielded my eyes, trying to see who was coming. At first I couldn't believe my eyes, but when the car stopped and Miss Beverly got out of the car, I couldn't deny it anymore. She had come to say goodbye.

With tears in her eyes, she wrapped her arms around me, whispering, "Why didn't you tell me? Why didn't you say goodbye?"

I just cried into her arms, overwhelmed by this woman's love, her efforts to find me to say goodbye. When the bus driver said we had to leave to make our flight, Miss Beverly shoved a piece of paper into my hand.

"Call me. Write me at my American address. Don't forget," she said.

After hugging me one last time, she watched as I boarded the bus and headed back to my seat. As the bus pulled away, I saw her watching me, waving. I waved back, and kept waving until I couldn't even see her outline on the horizon.

I thought about Miss Beverly for the rest of the bus ride. I hadn't met many Americans but the ones I had—the soldiers who brought me candy, my teacher John, Miss Beverly—treated me with kindness. As I traveled to their country, to America, I felt like I was traveling to a place where every person was as wonderful as the Americans I had already met.

When we arrived at the airport, I thanked the stars I was free of the bus, desperately hoping I wouldn't have to get on another one in America. But America—the idea, the culture, the geography—was so foreign to me. While Miss Beverly, my teacher John, and the classes at the PRPC camp had tried to prepare me for my new home, I understood only a small portion of what I was told, making America more like a fuzzy dream than a concrete idea in my mind. America was my family's dream, and it was finally coming true.

An immigration official led us to our gate, explaining to my parents that someone would be at LAX, the airport in Los Angeles, and would make sure we made our connecting flight. The immigration official explained that our refugee IDs must stay with each of us at all times because these little cards acted as the passports that would allow us into the United States.

My parents took this information to heart, telling us kids to stay close or "You might miss our flight." Má looked sternly at each of us in turn, focusing especially on me. "Don't let me catch you wandering off anywhere."

As my family, Chú Bảy's family, and the other refugees sprawled around the waiting area near our gate, two of my friends, Vu and Cuong, and I decided that two hours was long enough to go exploring. After all, Má said don't let her *catch* me—so I wouldn't. Although the guys and I had seen the airport when we had traveled through Manila to the PRPC, none of us had had a chance to explore the different levels and attractions. While our parents were distracted or dozing off, we snuck away, and I had one location in mind—the box that people had disappeared into the last time I had been in the airport. I remember Miss Beverly explaining once that the box took people places, but I couldn't remember what it was called. It didn't matter; I didn't need a name to figure out where it would take me.

Soon my friends and I spotted a group of people walking into the box, and we squeezed in quickly after them, afraid that the doors would crush us. The inside smelled like sweat and the tang of metal. I saw a wall of numbered buttons, some lit up from behind. But I didn't have long to study these because the doors soon opened and some of the people got out. We followed the mass of people out of the box, and it felt like we had entered a strange, alternate universe. Vu said, "This place must have a bunch of different floors."

Suddenly the airport seemed ten times bigger. How many floors could an airport have? As we walked around, we saw other gates and waiting areas similar to the one where we had left our families. Travelers lined up to buy food from different counters. Everyone was in a hurry. For a while we watched the boards of arrivals and departures, not quite sure what it meant.

Eventually, we decided we had better go back to our gate, but when we got back to the box, we had no idea what number to push. What floor had we come from? None of us knew. I tried not panic, staring around at my surroundings, which looked the same. Surrounded by Filipino people and signs, we couldn't ask anyone or read directions. I found a clock and checked the time before our plane left—we had one hour.

CHAPTER TEN

LOOKING AROUND FRANTICALLY, I SAW a woman standing behind a counter near one of the gates; she appeared to be answering travelers' questions. Perhaps the woman would speak English. Pointing at the woman, I told Vu and Cuong my plan, and we headed over. Never had I been so thankful for the hours of English classes I'd had. As slowly and carefully as I could, I used my best English to explain what had happened.

"We went in the box," I said, pointing. "We're lost. Where are we?"

She didn't understand, but I showed her my immigration ID and pointed back in the direction of the box.

"The elevator? You went on the elevator?" she said.

That's the word, I thought. *Elevator. What a strange word.*

After a few more minutes of stammered English words and hand gestures, she nodded, picked up a phone, and spoke over the loudspeaker. Before long, someone led the three of us back through the airport and to our waiting parents. As we approached the gate where our families waited, I caught sight of Má and Ba. They saw us coming, their faces flashing from worried to furious.

"That was so stupid of you! Do you want to get stuck here forever?" shouted Má. "Why would you worry your father and me like that? What if you had missed the flight?"

Ba looked at Má. "He knows. Don't yell so much," he said. "He made it back. He's okay."

I tried to explain that I hadn't meant to get lost, but for the rest of the time before our flight, Má made me sit in her sight at all times. Each time I shifted in my chair, she glared at me, as if to say, "Don't you dare." I stayed put. Given the choice, I would have been back exploring the airport, but I didn't dare provoke Má's wrath.

We boarded the plane, and my eyes nearly jumped from their sockets. I had thought our plane from Bangkok had been big, but this plane was bigger than a house—than several houses. *How would it even get off of the ground?* We got into our seats, and the plane rumbled to life, taking off in a fury of sound. After we took off, a woman startled me by handing out blankets and pillows to the passengers. *The stewardesses want us to be comfortable?* During our entire journey, people had gone out of their way to make us more miserable. These comforts must be part of a dream.

But I felt incredibly tired and, wrapping myself in my own blanket, soon I was fast asleep. When I woke up, another woman was offering me a tray of food, smiling as she handed it to me. "For you, sir," she said.

She didn't ask for money, and I stared at my food in confusion, like something might be written there to explain why I was given free food. After years of constant hunger, everything felt so surreal. What new life was this? My dream felt more like reality. *This must be what it feels like to go to America and become an American.*

We slept again, and ate again, but the plane still flew on. Loan and An grew restless, and Ba calmed them. "Hush, Loan. We'll be there soon," he said, smiling down at her. I tried to sit still and act mature, but I too began to feel restless. Was America really that far away?

A few hours later, we landed. "Welcome to Los Angeles International Airport," said a voice over the loudspeaker.

I felt excited, my entire body filled with energy. Suddenly I felt an urge to get off the plane. We were here—America!

LAX was the biggest airport I had ever seen—people were everywhere. If an immigration official had not met us as soon as we got off of the plane, I am sure we could have wandered around the airport for days. Thankfully, we had our guide, who explained that we had to catch another flight in a different terminal.

But weren't we already in the United States? I thought.

"You have to fly to Minnesota," the immigration official said. "And here, each of you needs a coat. It will be cold there."

She handed us each a jacket, each still in a plastic bag, and we held them out in front of us, like we had been given space suits. "Try it on," she said. The coats may have looked big, but they fit. Moving around in my new coat, I wondered, *What kind of cold would require such a warm piece of clothing?*

But we didn't have time to think about the coats much. Our guide gestured to us and began leading our family, and Chú Bảy's, through the airport and onto a bus that drove us to a different terminal, like we were maneuvering through a city rather than an airport. The immigration officer rushed everywhere, frantically checking the paper she held in her hand, looking up at signs, and turning back to make sure we were all accounted for. Ba told Má to hurry up because the airplane was leaving pretty soon, and Má ushered us forward, our group running through the terminals. We managed to keep up and soon were waiting in front of another gate. The other Vietnamese refugees had followed their own immigration officials to different gates around the airport. They were going to a different cities, but still in America.

As we waited, I tried to imagine the map of America in my head, but I couldn't quite remember how far Minnesota was from Los Angeles. But I didn't have long to find out. Soon we were on another plane, crammed into another group of seats. Though I slept on the plane, when we landed at the Minneapolis-Saint Paul International Airport, I felt as if we had been traveling for weeks, not just a couple of days. I looked out the window of the plane and guessed that it must be in the afternoon sometime, but my inner clock didn't know what time it was.

Again an immigration official met us as we exited the plane and led us to another gate. Ba asked the official how many flights we had, and the man said, "Bemidji is your next stop, so just one more flight."

"They must be sending us to the middle of nowhere," Chú Bảy said, laughing.

"At least they're not making us take the bus," said Ba.

I heard this was our last flight and felt incredible relief—we were almost there. In the waiting area by our gate, I saw that something strange was happening outside. A white powder-looking substance floated down from the sky and stuck to the thick layer of powder already on the ground. My siblings, cousins, and I plastered ourselves to the windows. What on earth was happening to the sky? Were pieces of it falling to the earth? While the other travelers in the airport appeared used to this phenomenon, I continued to crane my neck, looking into the thick, gray clouds over the runways. Ba came to the window.

"That must be fertilizer," he said. "Remember, we put something that looked similar on our rice fields back home." He paused. "In Vietnam."

Chủ Bảy joined him at the window. "Fertilizer? You think?" he said. "These Americans must be rich if they have so much fertilizer lying around. They must make a fortune selling to other countries."

As Ba and Chủ Bảy talked, my mind wandered back to the rice fields, to our familiar shack in Bà Ngoại's village. Two years was a long time, and I was beginning to forget. Faces were harder to remember, always swimming in and out of focus. Would I keep losing memories until I forgot what my family in Vietnam looked like? The Vietcong had treated us like animals, but the Americans treated us with such respect, welcoming us to our new home and our new lives.

The call for our plane to board interrupted our thoughts, and we got on the plane and found our seats. This airplane was much smaller than our last flight. Between our two families, we took up almost half the plane. It was a short flight to Bemidji, barely more than an hour. When we landed, instead of pulling up to the gate, a set of stairs was rolled up to the door of the plane. The moment the door opened, I felt real cold for the first time.

Our family's arrival in America

Remembering the jackets we had been given at LAX, I put mine on, but the cold still found its way to my face and hands. Quickly we walked to the terminal, desperate to get out of this foreign weather. At first I looked around for another immigration officer to appear and tell us where to go, but I didn't see one. Instead, a large crowd of people stood off to the side, holding signs with our names on them.

I was confused. Why did these strangers have signs with our names? But suddenly I saw Vietnamese faces among the crowd of white ones, and Chủ Sâu came forward to meet us. The entire throng of people surged forward with him, encircling and hugging us. "Welcome to America!" they said. There wasn't a dry eye around as stranger after stranger hugged my family and me. I couldn't be more thankful to be finally safe in this strange, cold land of Minnesota.

After our two groups had calmed down, Chủ Sâu introduced us to our sponsors, who beamed at us.

"There's a party waiting for you at the Lutheran church. Then we're going to take you to your new homes," said Chủ Sâu.

As we were heading to the parking lot, I turned to Chủ Sâu and asked, "Chủ Sâu, are the Americans rich because they have so much fertilizer?"

"What fertilizer, Tuần?" he said.

I pointed out at the white powder around the edges of the parking lot. "All of the white powder out there," I said.

Chủ Sâu laughed. "No, Tuần. It's snow, frozen water, not fertilizer," he said and continued to laugh as he reached down and picked up a hand-ful of snow and placed it in my hands.

"Cold," I said to myself, fixing the idea in my mind. The melting ice dripped over my numbing fingers. *This must be what Miss Beverly had been trying to explain to me,* I thought.

Thinking of Miss Beverly, I reached into my shorts for the slip of paper with her number and address. Maybe Chủ Sâu would know where she lived. It probably wasn't Minnesota, but maybe . . . I paused. Where was the paper? I tried my other pocket. Nothing. I tried my jacket pockets, hoping that I might have transferred the paper and had forgotten. I still couldn't find it and felt as numb as my fingers had holding the snow. Without the paper, I would never talk to Miss Beverly again. For days I would look for the paper, but I never found it.

—————————————

In the van, the air changed from frigid to comfortably warm. The van somehow controlled the temperature of the air. I looked around the car, trying to find out where the warm air came from and saw the vents in various places around the interior. Compared to the buses and vans in Vietnam, this van seemed like a vehicle of the future.

I watched the white world outside, wondering why it was so cold. When we got to the church, a crowd of people waited in the snow outside.

"Punch me, Trường," I said.

"What?" he said.

"Punch me. All these people are here for us? That can't be right," I said.

Trường laughed. "I was thinking the same thing."

At the party, tables and tables of food lined one wall, and Chủ Sâu took us around and named the different types of food. He said we could eat whatever we wanted and as much as we wanted.

It's really true about America. People really eat themselves to death, I thought. "Chủ Sâu, this could feed our entire village!"

Chủ Sâu laughed and said, "Yup, this is America."

I met more people than I could keep track of, each person smiling and hugging me. *Americans really are all as nice as Miss Beverly,* I thought.

After we had been at the church for awhile, I felt incredibly tired, the entire trip catching up with me. I asked Chủ Sâu, "Is our house very far from here?"

"It's down the road," he said.

In Vietnam, down the road meant traveling by boat or walking, a much longer trip than here in America where everyone drives. *At least it's not far then,* I thought.

Eventually, when everyone appeared as tired as I felt, Chủ Sâu said, "It's time to leave, so I'll go with Chủ Bảy, and Miss Jan and Miss Pam will take the rest of you to your house."

The trip from the church took twenty or thirty minutes, but to me the trip took no time at all. The world around me had captured my attention. We pulled up to a nice house right off the main street of Bemidji. Two of our sponsors, Miss Jan and Miss Pam, led us up through the screened porch and into the house. Compared to our many small apartments and our small house in Vietnam, this house was huge. Miss Pam first showed us the kitchen, opening a fridge full of food. Pointing at the different appliances, she named them and showed Má how they worked.

Miss Jan showed us the bathroom, which was inside the house. Turning the knob on the wall, water shot from the showerhead, falling down into the tub. Normally we washed ourselves from a bucket, scooping the water over our head. The bathroom was clean and modern; I had never seen a bathroom like this before, let alone used one. Was this real? When we got our own house, would we have a bathroom like this? The house felt like someone's home, lived in, with blankets on the beds and the kitchen fully stocked. I guessed that we were staying here until we found something more permanent.

Miss Jan and Miss Pam showed my parents the master bedroom while we kids wandered around our rooms. We wouldn't all have to share one room. After we had walked through the house and Miss Jan and Miss Pam had showed us how everything worked, we met back in the living room.

"I'll come back tomorrow to check on you," said Miss Pam. "Don't hesitate to ask us if you need anything. Our numbers are by the phone."

They both said goodbye and walked out the door leaving us alone in the house. All of us wanted to try the shower, so we took turns, everyone enjoying a hot shower for the first time. I couldn't get over how incredibly clean and expensive everything looked. I wondered over and over, *Do all Americans live like this?* Trường and I poked our heads outside and walked onto the porch, but Má called us back.

"Come back inside! We don't know what's out there. What if there's a curfew?" she said.

We weren't really disappointed; we discovered the television. One by one, we each wandered back into the living room, drawn like moths to the light of the TV. I could count on one hand how many times I had watched TV before, and my siblings had seen it far less. The images captured our attention; it didn't matter that we didn't understand what was being said. It was like we were looking into a piece of the future.

Ba sat in the recliner, Má sat on the couch with An, Phong, and Loan, and I sat on the floor with Trường. I looked around at my family, suddenly feeling a peace that I didn't recognize. *This is it. Finally we made it here together.* Closing my eyes, I tilted my head toward the ceiling. We had been fighting, surviving for so long, I couldn't believe that our journey was over. Every dark night taking care my siblings alone, the days at sea, the years in refugee camps—all of it had been for this moment and for every moment after, of safety and normality. I felt sure that I could never take for granted the sacrifices my parents had made so that my brothers, sister, and I could have lives of freedom away from the Vietcong.

Ba lit his cigarette and looked at all of us sitting around him, a satisfied smile spreading across his face. "We have made it. We have made it, kids. We are living in America now," he said. "This is our new life. We're Americans now. Always be grateful for what this country has done for us. They have given us another chance."

I don't remember ever seeing my father more emotional than he was that night. The Vietcong had taken everything from him, but the Americans had given it back—his dignity, his freedom, and a better chance for his children.

Looking back on that night, I would trade ten years of my life to relive that feeling—that everything would be okay from now on. The worst had to be behind us. But I soon learned that, even in the golden land of opportunity, life didn't always go as planned.

———

Like the rest of my family that night, I went to bed clean and happy, curling up on top of the bedclothes and feeling as if I was sleeping on the clouds. It was so hot in Vietnam that we didn't use blankets, so I had no idea that I could have pulled the top of the bed sheets back and slept underneath the covers. As I lay on my bed and drifted off to sleep, I wondered who had been so kind and let us stay in their house. How long were they going to be gone? I figured we'd find out soon enough.

Before I knew it, I was opening my eyes to the morning sun and the smell of cooking food. Má had found some long noodles in one of the cabinets and was cooking them with eggs, making an Americanized version of a fried noodle dish. After we had eaten, I sat at the kitchen table, staring at the wood trying to shake the feeling that I was still asleep. In the morning light, the house seemed more surreal than it had last night.

Looking outside, I caught sight of the snow on the ground. My brothers and I were drawn outside and we had our first snowball fight and discovered how to make different tracks in the snow.

That afternoon, Miss Pam and Miss Jan returned to check on us.

"Did you get enough to eat?" asked Miss Pam, opening the fridge and peering inside.

Our family in front of our new home

Má nodded, but neither sponsor appeared convinced.

"Then why does it look like you've barely eaten anything?" asked Miss Jan.

Má tried to explain that she didn't want to take too much food. What would the owners of the house think when they came back?

Miss Jan and Miss Pam smiled, giving each other a significant glance. Miss Pam reopened the fridge. "See this?" she said. "This is all yours." She gestured to the entire kitchen. "All of this is yours too. This is *your* home."

Má was speechless, her eyes wet and shining.

Later that evening, Chú Sâu and Chú Bảy brought their families to our house, like they used to in Vietnam. Our tradition held that the younger brothers would gather at the eldest brother's house, and this was the first time we had gotten together with Chú Sâu since he left Vietnam four years ago.

Chú Sâu and Chú Bay's families
at our house

A festive atmosphere filled the house as we celebrated our spontaneous holiday. Má and my aunts cooked so much food that we couldn't eat it all. After dinner, the men invited me to sit with them in the living room to talk about the good old days in Vietnam. I sat on the edge of the couch, listening to their conversation and hoping that no one would bring up the fight Ba and Chú Sâu had while we were still in Sikhiu. But, thankfully, no one mentioned it, and the night continued with everyone in good spirits.

We had many new experiences to wrap our minds around. One of our sponsors, Miss Donna, was the minister's wife at the Lutheran church in town. The first Sunday after we arrived, Miss Donna picked us up and took us to church. We had never been to church before and could barely understand what the preacher was saying, but we enjoyed the ritual nature of

Má and Miss Donna

the service. There wasn't a temple in Bemidji, but we felt a comfort going to a place of worship.

Miss Donna also helped my siblings and me register for school, which we were entering mid-semester. Since my father had told the immigration officials that we were all two years younger than we were, I was placed in ninth grade at age seventeen. But I looked young enough that no one questioned my age.

Before my family got a car, Miss Jan, Miss Donna, and Miss Pam drove my family to doctor's appointments, the DMV, and anywhere else we might need to go. But when the sponsors learned that Ba was a good mechanic, they found a used truck for him to fix up. In a couple of weeks, Ba had it up and running.

Though Ba already knew how to drive, he didn't know America's driving laws. Chủ Sâu took him on the road to practice, explaining how the roads worked and what the various traffic signs meant. But Ba still had to pass the written test and the manual was written in English. Ba studied the booklet, but the language barrier proved frustrating, causing him to fail twice. Chủ Sâu teased that Ba had to pass the next time, or the DMV would require a mandatory waiting period. But Ba passed, quickly putting an end to Chủ Sâu's jives. With the truck came a new independence from our sponsors. While they still helped us when we needed it, we no longer depended on them for transportation, which made my family more confident in our new life in Bemidji.

While Ba was fixing the truck and getting his driver's license, my brothers, sister, and I had to adjust to a new school. Though I had thought that the school in the Philippines was large and modern, I had never seen a school like the high school in Bemidji. I had never had so many classes in different rooms before, and bells rang constantly, sending students scurrying in different directions. But the other students, especially the other Vietnamese students, helped me out, making sure I found my classes and understood what the teachers were saying.

At lunch, I would sit at the lunch table, dipping my French fries in fish sauce and enjoying the disgusted looks on the American students' faces. Inevitably, someone at lunch would say, "Speak Vietnamese!" So my friends and I would teach them rude words instead of the simple "Hello" and "Thank You" that they requested to learn. We'd laugh as they walked around saying the wrong words, so proud of themselves that they had learned a couple words in Vietnamese.

We had arrived in America in March of '86. The snow was thick on the ground, and it still hadn't melted by the spring, a few months later. Most of the time, my brother Trường and I avoided the cold by taking the bus, or Ba would drive us to school. But one time, the truck broke down, and Trường and I had to run the rest of the way to school, terrified our teachers would punish us for being late. We didn't know that American public schools didn't beat kids for being late. As soon as I realized that we wouldn't have been punished, I wished that I had stayed behind to help Ba with the truck. I hated the idea of Ba out in the cold on his own.

After the truck broke down, Trường and I had to walk to school if we missed the bus. One time we missed the bus and had to walk home, but we passed our street, not noticing it underneath the masses of snow. Every house and street looked the same, the only difference being the street names and the house numbers. But what was our house number? Neither of us knew. Chú Sâu had given us his number for such an occasion, so we hurried to a pay phone, searching every pocket and corner of our bags for change.

Finally we counted out enough coins and my numb fingers shoved the coins into the slot. With chattering teeth, we described our location to Chủ Sâu, who said he would pick us up soon.

Trường and I huddled together on the snowy curb for half an hour before our uncle picked us up. Chủ Sâu pulled up to the curb, and we hurried into the car, and, two blocks later, were being dropped off again.

"What?" I said. "We could have been home already!"

Chủ Sâu laughed and said, "I bet you'll never forget your house number now, huh?"

He was right.

While the snow had enchanted us at first, Trường, Phong, and I quickly came to hate the snow. Rather than go outside after school, we would stay inside in front of the TV, watching hours of Vietnamese dubbed kung-fu movies Chủ Sâu gave us. We had never seen movies that captured our attention like those films. Their magical stories seemed so close to the myths Ba and Ông Nội had told us when we were kids.

While we kids struggled with the cold, Ba and Má struggled the most with the cold. They also struggled to find work. Ba tried to help the family any way he could. After he got his driver's license, Ba would take us older boys to a nearby lake where he had seen men ice fishing. The fishermen would leave the fish they caught out on the ice, like they were leaving them there to die. Ba couldn't believe the waste he was seeing, so he would go down to the lake, take the fish, and bring them home for us to eat.

One time, Ba went to pick up the fish, and one of the fisherman ran up, demanding to know what he was doing. Ba explained that he was picking up the fish and taking them home so they wouldn't be wasted. The fisherman laughed and explained that the fishermen left the fish on the ice so that the fish would freeze and the men would pick them up later. Ba, mortified, quickly apologized, but the man waved him off, still chuckling to himself.

Ba and Chú Bảy did manage to find a few temporary jobs as janitors, but nothing consistent. Eventually Má and Ba learned of a company called "The Lady's Slipper," which sold random knickknacks. After picking up material for stuffed animals and decorative bird houses, they would assemble them at home. Má recruited us to help her, and Ba and our uncles often walked in to find three teenage boys sitting in front of the TV, stuffing bears while watching martial arts movie marathons.

A couple months after we arrived, Miss Pam's husband, Mr. Mike, brought me to his jewelry store downtown to teach me how to work with jewelry. The names and cuts of the gems fascinated me, and I quickly learned how to carefully handle and clean the pieces of

Má stuffing animals for "Lady Slipper" and An doing homework

jewelry. After a week of lessons, Mr. Mike paid me fifty dollars.

"Oh, no, Mr. Mike," I said. "I'm still learning. I haven't even really started working yet."

But Mr. Mike insisted, so I thanked him and biked straight to the grocery store. I bought a box of wrapped, chocolate-dipped ice cream cones, a frozen pizza, and two-liter of Coke, hanging the bags

Mr. Don teaching me jewelry work

on my handlebars as I made my way home. When I got home, my parents eyed me with suspicion.

"Where'd you get that food?" asked Má.

"Mr. Mike paid me today," I said.

"But you haven't done any work. He's still teaching you," she said, eyes narrowing.

I shrugged. "He insisted."

I called Chủ Sâu and asked him to take me to Pamida, our local version of a superstore, to get a cassette player and a new pair of shoes. Though I quickly found the shoes I wanted, I didn't know that the shoes came in different sizes. Since I didn't know I could take them back either, I stuffed rolled-up socks in the toes of the shoes and wore the shoes to school, insisting to my friends that my feet really were *that* big.

———————

In spring of 1987, about a year after we had arrived in Bemidji, Chủ Sâu moved to San Jose, California, to find better work—and warmer weather. After Chủ Sâu left, Ba and Chủ Bảy began to talk about leaving Minnesota too. Bemidji was too cold, and they couldn't find any work because of the language barrier. A distant cousin called and told Ba about the large Vietnamese community in Louisiana, and Ba and Chủ Bảy jumped at the chance. But I didn't want to leave my new school, my new friends, or my new life.

Though Ba decided to let me stay and finish out high school in Bemidji, I was legally underage and needed to stay with a legal guardian. After asking around, Thiem Sâu's sister-in-law Hanh, agreed to let me stay with her and her boyfriend, Ngan. By July, Ba finalized the moving plans, and left with Chủ Bảy and their families. Although I hated saying goodbye, I was a man now. I felt sure I could take care of myself, but Ngan, Hanh, and I didn't get along. Even with the start of school keeping me out of the house, I fought constantly with Hanh's boyfriend. I still worked for Mr. Mike, trying to make what money I could, but I hated going home.

Later that fall, my friend Loi had heard enough complaining about Hanh and Ngan.

"If you hate them so much, why don't you come stay at my house," he said. "My foster parents wouldn't mind."

My room at the Granger's house

I knew Loi had come to America as an orphan and was taken in by Mr. and Mrs. Granger, who loved him like their own son. I still wasn't sure I should leave Hanh's place, but when Ngan started accusing me of stealing, I knew I had to move out.

That Christmas, I woke up at the Grangers to Loi shouting, "Wake up, Tuần! It's Christmas!"

Bleary-eyed, I rolled out of bed. The other kids at school had talked incessantly about what they wanted for Christmas. Despite my attempts to steer the conversation towards something—anything—else, the excitement of the upcoming holiday would overrule any other topics.

I wasn't expecting anything for Christmas, so why get my hopes up? But as I walked into the living room, the Grangers stood by the tree shouting, "Merry Christmas!"

"Your presents are over here, Tuần," said Mrs. Granger, beaming.

I paused. "Really? For me?" I said.

She kept beaming and ushered me towards the tree. "Of course," she said. "You think we'd forget Christmas?"

That year I experienced the joy of Christmas for the first time—my first real Christmas. From that day, Mr. and Mrs. Granger became Mom and Dad Granger, and the feeling was mutual. Mom Granger washed my laundry, insisting that I complete my homework before I helped around the house. Around the dinner table, Mom and Dad Granger insisted that I use good grammar and would correct my English no matter how small the mistake. Immersed in an English-only household, my English grew better every day, and I gained confidence at school, my grades improving since I could understand more of the material.

By March, a year after my family and I had arrived in the United States, I had merged seamlessly with the household, thriving underneath the love and support of the Grangers.

"Tuấn, it's your brother on the phone!" called out Mom Granger one afternoon.

I came to the phone and held it to my ear, "Yes?"

"Anh Hai? Brother?" said the voice at the other end. "Anh Hai, this is Trường."

Trường still used the respectful title used for the oldest son. "Oh, hey. What's going on?" I said, expecting the usual news from my family in Louisiana.

"I don't how to say this, so I am just going to go ahead and say it," he said. "It's Loan. She's sick."

"What? Does she have the flu?"

"No, it's not like that," he said. "I mean, she's got a brain tumor. The doctor says he can't do anything else."

My brain froze. This couldn't be right. I had just seen her nine months ago. She couldn't have gotten sick this fast—not in America. "Trường, this can't be right. Ba or Má would have said something."

Trường paused at the other end before finally answering, "They didn't want to worry you. But I couldn't wait anymore. It's time for you to come home."

CHAPTER ELEVEN

SITTING ON THE PLANE HEADING to Louisiana, I kept repeating to myself what Trường had said on the phone: "She has a brain tumor. The doctor says she doesn't have much time."

In Vietnam she would die, but surely the American doctors can help her, I thought.

When I landed in New Orleans, Ba and Chủ Bảy picked me up from the airport. We drove to the hospital, the horror of the situation draining any desire for conversation. But after a few minutes, the silence sat thick and heavy around us, making the atmosphere awkward and uncomfortable.

"Nice of Mr. and Mrs. Granger to buy a ticket for you to fly home," said Chủ Bảy. I nodded. The Grangers had been wonderful, letting me talk through the situation and explaining what a brain tumor was and how, even in America, brain tumors were still deadly. But as we headed to the hospital, I still felt like this couldn't be real, like I couldn't wake from a nightmare.

"Your sister has been asking about you," said Ba. "She's going to be happy to see you home."

When we arrived at the hospital, Ba and Chu Bảy led me out into the sticky heat and through the sterile halls of the hospital with a robotic familiarity, and I tried not to think about how many times Ba must have found his way through this maze of corridors.

We slowed at the door to one of the rooms, Ba gesturing for me to go inside. Though I hadn't known what to expect, I'd never imagined that I wouldn't even recognize my sister. The little girl I'd known had disappeared, leaving behind a stranger in her place. She had a thick layer of fat from the medicine she had been on, and patches of her hair were missing after having been shaved off for a recent surgery. Tubes led from various parts of her body to the machines around her. I held my breath, still hoping that this girl couldn't be my sister, that it was a horrible mistake.

"Brother," she said. "You came. You came home."

When she opened her mouth, her voice was Loan's, and I knew I couldn't deny it anymore. I couldn't control the tears coming out of my eyes. I cried for the horrible disease killing my sister, for the time lost when I hadn't known, and for failing to protect her. I told her I was sorry that I hadn't been here to help her. I could have helped translate for Má or maybe helped her when she was sick. She just smiled and said, "You're here now."

We left the hospital and drove the hour to Houma, Louisiana, a small town an hour outside of New Orleans. When we reached my parents' apartment, again I thought there must be some sort of mistake. The apartment complex was run down, in a neighborhood equally as destitute. After Má and my brothers greeted me at the door, I sat down at the kitchen table, listening to all that had happened in the last nine months.

When Ba and Chú Bảy had made their survey trip to Houma to figure out where their families were going to live , they had somehow lost their contact's number and were stuck penniless in an unfamiliar town. They had spent that first night under a bridge, trying to figure out what to do next. The following day, another Vietnamese man had found them and helped them find the Vietnamese community, housing, and food. The housing looked questionable at best, but they had felt that it was enough.

After they had moved their families to Houma, Ba and Chủ Bảy began working on shrimping boats, and Má and Thiem Bảy began working at a crab processing plant, learning how to crack apart legs and claws to quickly harvest the meat. Soon after they had settled in, Loan began to have horrible headaches. At first Má though it was something that would pass, but Loan's headaches occurred more frequently. Má decided this couldn't wait.

Taking the day off of work, Má found a clinic that took Medicaid and waited all day for Loan to see the doctor. When the doctor finally examined Loan, he dismissed her complaints, saying she was exaggerating. Just give her Tylenol, he said. Má did what the doctor had said, but Loan's headaches intensified. She began throwing up—every sound and source of light an agony to her. When Má took Loan back to the doctor, he again dismissed Loan's symptoms.

It wasn't until Loan blacked out and fell down the stairs that the doctor ordered a series of tests. He found the tumor, but by then it was too late. Má took Loan to a specialist who ordered chemotherapy and radiation to try to shrink the tumor, but nothing helped; anything they tried seemed to do more harm than good.

Loan and An

"That's when Trường called you," said Má, signaling the end of the story. "We told him not to, but you're here now. Maybe that will help."

I felt so numb. *The doctors ignored Loan for so long. What if they had taken her seriously? Would she be dying right now?* Anger flooded my entire body. They would *never* get away with anything like that again. She was my baby sister. I would take care of her now.

"You will have to stay with Loan as much as you can," said Má. "I need to work. We can't afford for me to stay with Loan all of the time, and Trường has missed too much school."

At the mention of school, Trường rolled his eyes.

"Just wait until you see the school, Tuần. You won't be sad to miss it either," he said.

"Is it really that bad?" I asked.

"Wait. You'll see," he said. "You'll see."

Trường didn't know how right he was. I went to the registration office at the school, which seemed older and less clean than my school in Minnesota. That afternoon in the library, I tried to figure out my homework, but three big guys kept eyeing me, walking back and forth in front of my table. I tried not to look like they bothered me, but as soon as they left the library, I hurried out of the room and made for the bathroom. Inside, cigarette smoke filled the air, causing me to duck my head and cough, my lungs searching for oxygen.

I looked up and saw the three large boys standing around the sinks. The biggest one pulled a cigarette from his lips, blowing smoke in my direction.

"What do you want?" said the big guy.

"I want to use the bathroom," I said.

The big guy swore at me and told me in no uncertain terms that I needed to leave.

"What did you say?" I said, narrowing my eyes.

He swore at me again, threw down his cigarette as he stepped towards me to give me a shove. I punched him. It may have been a few years since my martial arts training, but I still could take these guys down. I dodged the other two guys and pushed them into stalls. I picked up the big guy like he was nothing and stuffed him butt-first into a large barrel trash can.

———

Someone called me into the principal's office where he was waiting for me with a Vietnamese girl. The girl turned to me and said, "Hey, I'm Lisa.

I nodded. "Tuấn," I said.

"Right." She wasn't perturbed at my rudeness. "I'm here to translate."

"I can speak English."

"But he can't understand what you're saying," said Lisa.

I didn't respond.

She spoke back to the principal in an almost accentless English, which I knew must mean she had grown up most of her life in America.

Ignoring Lisa, I told the principal why I had fought the three other students. "Then you should have told me or a teacher. You can't fight every guy that insults you. Violence is not tolerated in this school, son," he said. "I understand today was your first day, and it can be hard for people like—well, for new students to fit in."

I paused, narrowing my eyes at the man. *People like what? What does he mean by that?* I thought. But I didn't have a chance to dwell on it long. The principal sent me out of his office with a warning to never fight again.

Lisa left with me and I asked, "What did he mean back there?"

"What do you mean?" said Lisa.

"The way the principal was back there. People like us?" I said.

"Oh," she shrugged. "Some people don't like us," she said but didn't elaborate.

Before I left Bemidji, Mom Granger had warned me that I may have problems in Louisiana. "The people down there can be incredibly racist, Tuấn. So be careful."

Heading home that day, I realized I had experienced the racism Mom Granger had warned me about. Not the casual everyday, passive looks that I experienced in Minnesota, but aggressive racism that made me afraid to go back to school. Hurtful phrases like "you people" and "people like you" had even come out of my teachers' mouths. These phrases were reminders that I wasn't from here, that I was different. For the first time since stepping off the plane in Minnesota, I felt like I didn't belong in America.

A few days later, the school bus reached my stop, and I got up to get off. But at the door, a guy stood in my way.

"I heard what you did to Abe," he said.

"What?" I said.

"You think you're so great, shoving Abe in the trash can."

"I want to get off of the bus."

The bus driver yelled, "Roland, shut up and let that kid out!"

But Roland ignored her, shoving me. I exploded, hitting Roland back and sending him flying into the laps of two girls in the front seat behind the driver. One of the girls was Lisa. She yelled at us as Roland found his footing and started fighting again.

When the fight was over, the bus driver yelled at us, closed the doors, and drove us back to school. She got the principal. He was not happy.

Our life settled into a routine: I would go to school and stay with Loan on the evenings and weekends while Má got in as many hours at work as she could. Trường watched Phong and An, trying to make sure they had enough to eat and did their homework. At school, my tendency to get into fights got me the nickname, "Chuck Norris," which stuck with me. Every time I got in trouble, Lisa would be there, translating the principal's disapproval and punishments for my constant violence. I missed school a lot too, trying to give Má a chance to get more hours at work, but the school year ended before the principal noticed the situation. I welcomed the coming summer as a reprieve from constant fighting.

The girls at school were the only ones impressed by how I managed to win so many fights and tried to get my attention. But with Loan still in the hospital, I didn't care about girls. Besides, I was still talking to a girl up in Minnesota, hoping that maybe Loan would get better and I could go back. I called Mom Granger and talked about how miserable I felt in Louisiana. At the end of every conversation, she would say, "Whenever you want to come home, just say the word and we'll buy you a ticket. Any time. Really."

But we both knew I couldn't go back to Bemidji with Loan in the hospital. My family needed me right now. That summer, Loan was released from the hospital and came home, but the doctor still said she was living on borrowed time. As the summer grew hotter, our house became an oven, compressing the humid air and making Loan more miserable than ever. I thought of the air conditioned hospital and thought it might have been better if she had stayed there, but at least now Má could work full time.

Má and Ba had been saving for a while and that summer managed to buy a shrimping boat. Chủ Bảy and Thiem Bảy also bought a shrimping boat, so they began to work longer hours out on the ocean. I helped them when I could, but I hated the miserable work. Midsummer, Ba and Chủ Bảy decided that the families should visit Chủ Sâu in San Jose. They took the seats out of an old minivan so everyone could travel together in the same vehicle.

I would have gone with them, but someone needed to stay behind to take care of the boats. I was thankful I didn't have to travel across the country in a cramped van that didn't have air conditioning. But Má wouldn't leave Loan with me, insisting that she go to San Jose with the rest of the family. Má knew Loan didn't have much time and wanted her to experience as much of America as she could. But I hated the idea of Loan traveling in that miserable vehicle.

School started up again in the fall, and I began my junior year with dread. Loan didn't get better. She occasionally had to make trips to the hospital when her health would take a turn for the worse, but Loan always got better and came home. Lisa lived in the same apartment complex as we did and had become Loan's friend before I even moved down to Louisiana. When she wasn't translating for me in the principal's office, she was visiting Loan, who now usually stayed in the house.

That Halloween, I was working on Ba's car in the parking space in front of our apartment and saw An and my cousins running off to go trick-or-treating with Lisa's cousin, Kim Loan. Kids from Lisa and Kim Loan's family joined the group too, making a large herd of costumed, screaming children. Shaking my head, I was about to get back to work when I saw Lisa running from her apartment across the parking lot. She held her hand like it was injured. She came out of her aunt's apartment, and I asked, "What's up with your hand?"

"It got shut in a door. Just a cut. We didn't have any first-aid supplies," she said distractedly. "Did you see Kim Loan? And some kids? I was supposed to help take them trick-or-treating."

"You mean the army of screaming ghosts and who knows what else? Yeah, they went down the street."

"Which way?"

I shrugged. "I'm not sure."

"Oh," she said, looking unsure of what to do.

I asked her if she always watched kids, and she said that she watched them all the time. Her family was Catholic, so she had a lot of brothers and sisters, but two of them were still in Vietnam. I asked why they didn't come with the rest of her family, and she told me how her mother had been forced to leave them behind when the family fled Vietnam or none of

them would have gotten out of the country. She told the story like it was nothing, but I knew the pain that was behind the casual voice. I had heard so many of these stories since fleeing Vietnam.

"She was out of the house with me at the time, and if she had gone back to get my brother and sister, it would have been too late," she said.

We talked for a long time until I finally said, "Hey, I need to go to the store to get some car parts."

Tuần and Lisa

"Okay, I'll go with you," she said. And she did.

After that night, we were inseparable. But as a strong Catholic, Lisa's dad would never approve of her dating a boy from a Buddhist family, so we kept our relationship a secret, hanging out in groups and showing no signs of affections in public. One time, I rode with Lisa and Kim Loan to take their friend Carrie home. Lisa dropped off Kim Loan too, to give us a chance to be alone. We were parked in the one of the spaces in front of Lisa's apartment when her dad came out of the house.

"Quick! Crawl in the foot space," she said.

So I curled up underneath the dashboard of the passenger side of the car, making myself as small as possible. Her dad came out, and I heard him saying something to Lisa and her responding in a nonchalant tone. Footsteps came closer to the car. "I know you're seeing someone Lisa. Is he in there?" said Lisa's dad. He peered into the car, but must not have seen me, because he left with Lisa to go back into their apartment.

We successfully hid our relationship for awhile, but at the end of that school year, Lisa's dad caught us in the library. He didn't talk to Lisa for months. In traditional Vietnamese fashion, my parents went to talk to Lisa's parents, trying to convince them that all four parents needed to support my match with Lisa. But Lisa's dad refused to approve our relationship, saying that no Catholic daughter of his would date and marry a Buddhist. My parents didn't understand why Lisa and I couldn't keep our own separate religions, but they could see Lisa's dad wasn't budging.

No matter what Lisa's dad said, I loved Lisa. I hadn't expected it to happen, but Lisa was different than any other girl I'd met. Her mind was so sharp and she hadn't fawned over me like other girls. She made me feel like I needed to become my best self to deserve her attentions. She helped me become a better person, and I wanted to spend the rest of my life thanking her for that.

Loan's health took a turn for the worse, and the doctor told my parents that she needed to go into hospice. I hated the hospice center and didn't want her to have to be alone, but the principal said that if I missed any more days of school, I would be expelled. One day I visited Loan and found the nurses were transferring her to a new bed. It looked to me like they tossed her around carelessly. Cursing at them, I yelled, "She's a human being, not some kind of stuffed animal. You will *not* treat her like this!"

Thankfully, Loan wasn't there much longer. She passed away that spring, in April of 1989, about a year after I had moved down from Minnesota. When our sponsor, Miss Donna, heard that Loan had died, she flew down from Minnesota to help with the funeral. Má appreciated the help; our family was a mess, but no one more than Ba. From the first time he had seen her after he had been released from the prison camp, Loan had captured his heart. A parent should never have to bury his child, and Ba had to bury his princess.

Because of how Loan's death day and my birthday misaligned, Má wouldn't let me go to the funeral. According to Vietnamese superstition, I might die, or one of my brothers. Though I was angry that she wouldn't let me go because of a superstition I didn't even understand, Má had just lost her only daughter. I didn't want her to be afraid of losing a son too.

After Loan passed, I couldn't stand the pain. After everything that we had been through, Loan hadn't died out on the ocean or in a refugee camp. She had died in America. I began to use alcohol and drugs to dull my feelings, as I desperately wanted relief. With every drink or drug, I felt a little less of the crushing pain I had come to recognize as my life.

In June, Lisa came to me with terrible news: her father was moving them to Guam to be closer to her grandfather. The news came suddenly and I thought, *This. This is my life. If a bad thing can happen, it will.* But I loved Lisa. For the first time, I truly had fallen in love. I had been right to love her. I knew the moment I started dating this Vietnamese girl that I wouldn't date anyone else.

Before she left for Guam, I wanted to give Lisa something to remember me by. Phone calls and letters would be difficult from so far away, so I bought a book, I didn't care what kind, and wrote notes on random pages throughout the book. Lisa was always reading something, so her parents would never suspect that I was communicating to her with a book.

After she left, I had to take summer school and was gone most of the day. I wrote Lisa letters when I could, but her replies took so long to come back. Finally, I got a letter from Lisa saying that she had tried to call me, but Má had answered.

Your mother said you weren't answering the phone because you didn't love me anymore. She said we should give up because our families are too different and I am so far away. Is she right? Have you given up? I wrote her back immediately. I still loved her.

With Lisa gone, I desperately wanted to leave Houma and move back to Bemidji. Bemidji held so many wonderful memories for me. Houma held nothing but this pain I couldn't escape. Loan was gone, and now Lisa. I had to leave.

Before I could figure out how to move, Lisa wrote and let me know that her grandfather had died, so her dad had changed his mind and they were moving back to Houma. I couldn't believe it; as quickly as she had left, she was coming home. While I was thrilled, I still hated Houma. Lisa came back, but I still felt miserable. In the fall after school started, I got into a gang fight, and the principal expelled me from school. I had found my way out of Houma.

———————————

I moved back to Bemidji that fall, planning to go back to my old high school and graduate next spring with the class of 1990. At first I stayed with the Grangers, but soon Loi and I moved into our own place with Loi's friend Thong. Mr. Mike let me work at the jewelry store again and I picked up odd jobs around town to make some extra money. Though I felt that I was doing much better in Bemidji, my move was the hardest on Lisa. She had begged me not to leave her when she had just moved back to the States, but I knew I needed to get away from my old friends, the drugs, and alcohol.

By the spring of 1990, I was finally getting ready to graduate. I couldn't believe that after everything that had happened at my old school, I had turned things around enough to graduate on time.

One weekend in May, my friends and I went bowling. Around midnight, I felt odd, an uncomfortable feeling in my gut that wouldn't let me go.

"Hey guys, let's go home. I think I'm done for the night," I said.

Loi, Thong, and I went home sitting around our living room drinking beer, winding down before we went to bed. The phone rang.

I picked it up. "Hello?"

"Tuần? Is this Tuần?" said the voice at the other end.

"Yes"

"Oh, Tuần," said the voice. I could tell the person on the other end was female, familiar, and crying.

"This is Thiem Bảy. There's been a terrible accident."

I started when I recognized my aunt's voice. "Accident?"

"Your father's dead. They could all be dead. I just don't know."

"What?" My hand holding the phone went numb and I almost dropped the receiver. "What? Did you say?"

"Trường was driving the car. Everybody was in it. He fell asleep and the car hit a tree. I heard someone was lifeflighted to a hospital, but I am not sure who."

Buzzing rang in my ears like it had during that first explosion in Cần Thơ. I felt numb and disoriented. I heard something, someone saying my name.

"Tuấn? You there?" said Thiem Bảy.

"Yes," I mumbled. "I'm—I'm coming."

After I hung up the phone, Thong and Loi asked what was going on. I told my friends, Loi got on the phone with the airport, but the next flight out wasn't until the next morning. My friend tried to calm me down, telling me it was okay. But it wasn't okay. I wasn't sure if it would ever be okay again.

———————

For the second time I sat on a plane, hurrying to Louisiana after hearing horrible news. Words repeating over and over in my head: *Your father's dead. They could all be dead.* Trường had been driving. Suddenly consumed by my worry and anger, I felt sure I was going to let him have it when I got down there. If he was okay that is. My heart sunk further down into my stomach, making me feel sick with anxiety. I had no idea what kind of situation would greet me after I got off of the plane. What was I stepping into? Would anyone be left alive when I made it to Houma?

Chủ Bảy picked me up at the airport with Chủ Sâu, who had already flown in from California. As soon as I saw my uncles in the terminal, I begged them for every detail. Was my family alive? What happened?

Chủ Bảy began to explain as we headed out to the car, not wanting to waste any time. "Your mother and brothers were a little banged up, but nothing worse than a few stitches. But your father," he paused before going on. "Your father's on a ventilator. The doctor says he's brain dead."

Brain dead, I thought repeating the news to myself over and over. Chủ Bảy explained that when Trường had fallen asleep and hit the tree, Phong had been in the passenger seat, Ba and Má sitting in the back seat of the car with An between them. At the moment of impact, Ba had wrapped himself around An, exposing his head to the gap between the two front seats, but Ba had been thrown forward, the gear shift entering Ba's eye socket and into his brain. I didn't want to hear this part. It was too much, and I tried to hold myself together.

"You're the man of the house now, Tuần. You have to be strong for your mother and brothers," said Chủ Sâu.

I nodded, trying not to think about what that meant. Ba had said the very same thing to me each time he was on assignment during the war and when the Vietcong took him away to the prison camp. I remembered Ba telling me after my grandfather's funeral that real men don't cry, and I held it together.

We got to the hospital, and my uncles led me to a room in ICU where a man I did not recognize as my father lay on the hospital bed, his life now more machine than man. His face and head were swathed in bandages, bruises spreading across every visible part of his body. For a moment, I thought I saw Ông Nội's mutilated face torn apart by the land mine in the bed, but slowly I saw Ba beneath the bandages. Sitting by his bed, I watched as the ventilator forced air in and out of his lungs, keeping his body just barely alive. Images of Loan in the hospital flashed behind my eyes, reminding me what my family had already suffered.

I cried then. I cried for his impaled body, that I hadn't been there to take care of my family because I had left. The last time I had seen my father, we argued about me leaving for Bemidji. He wanted me to stay; the family needed me. But I had refused to stay and left my parents right after they had lost their only daughter. When she died, it was as if they had lost their oldest son too.

Never in my life had I felt like this, felt that sorrow and pain would consume me—killing me too. After Loan died, her absence left a constant ache, like I was missing a piece of my heart. But with Ba, my heart disintegrated, collapsed in on itself. I kept thinking, *This was not supposed to happen. Not in America.* My father didn't even have a chance to live the American dream, to finally be at peace. Now it was too late.

The doctor told my family that Ba was all but dead and that we needed to decide whether or not to take him off of the ventilator. The doctor said we could take our time deciding what we wanted to do. At first Má was resolute—there must be something the doctor could do to save him. But, after a few days, Má realized we didn't have the money to keep Ba alive. As the doctor said, Ba was already dead.

The day before the doctor took Ba off of the ventilator, I visited Ba in the hospital. I talked to Ba for a few hours, knowing he had to be listening somehow. I told Ba about Minnesota, about how much I loved it there. I told him how I was sorry that he didn't have a chance to learn to love

America like I did, to experience everything our new country had to offer. I told him I would experience life enough for the both of us, but I sure wished he would be here to see it instead.

After I said my final goodbyes, I left the hospital and bought a new suit for Ba to be cremated in, but I didn't go to the hospital the day he passed. After Ba was cremated, Má put his ashes in the temple, asking the monks to pray for Ba's spirit.

A few weeks after the funeral, I took Ba's place on the shrimping boats. Having missed my graduation, I received my diploma in the mail. Though I worked hard, almost every cent I earned I threw away on more drugs and alcohol. Lisa tried to comfort me, insisting that I shouldn't give up and that I should still apply to college.

"What college would take me? Where would I go?" I said.

"What about Bemidji State? You love it up there," she said.

I knew that by suggesting I leave Louisiana, Lisa must really want this for me. Why else would she suggest that I leave her? Steeling myself for failure, I applied, not putting too much hope in me getting into the school. When my acceptance letter came in the mail, I couldn't believe it. Wasn't everything in my life supposed to go wrong? I told Lisa, and she threw her arms around me, showing the enthusiasm that I couldn't muster.

"You are going to go, right?" she said. "You have to. It says you even got financial aid."

I still couldn't believe it. "But what about you? I can't leave you behind."

She shrugged, trying not to spoil my joy. "No, I can't leave you. Come with me," I said.

Lisa looked startled, "What?"

"Run away with me."

"My parents would never allow it."

"We could run away together and they couldn't do a thing about it. We could be together in Minnesota. I am not leaving you this time, and we have no chance if we stay in Louisiana."

It took awhile, but eventually I convinced Lisa to come with me and we began to make plans.

I kept working on the shrimping boats, now saving as much as I could. To not draw suspicion, Lisa and I pretended that we had broken up and avoided each other in public. Near the end of the summer, I drove Lisa to a friend's house and she called her parents to tell them that they had made her lose the love of her life, so she was running away to New Orleans. After dropping Lisa off, I went out on a shrimping boat for a couple of weeks like I had been doing for months. When I returned, I picked up Lisa and we drove to Bemidji.

Tuần and Lisa

In Bemidji we found an apartment and Lisa called her high school in Houma, to tell them that her father had decided to pick up at a moment's notice and move, like he had when they moved to Guam. Asking no questions, the school transferred her school records as she asked. It had worked; we had made it to Bemidji.

I started classes in the fall, taking a full load and working as much as I could. In the morning, I worked at a grocery store from 4AM until my classes began at 8AM. By the end of the school year, Lisa had graduated as a member of the class of 1991 and I had passed my first-year classes at Bemidji State University.

Then we got a call from one of Lisa's sisters. Lisa's two sibling who had been left in Vietnam had come to the United States. Though Lisa wanted to go back to Houma, she knew her father would never allow her to come home.

"What if I converted to Catholicism? He couldn't be upset about us getting married then, right?" I said.

"You'd do that?" she said. She knew that in our culture, it was the woman who takes up the practices and joins the family of her husband. It would dishonor the man if he took up his wife's religion. But I didn't care. Lisa had left her entire family for me. How could I not do this thing for her, for us?

We returned to Louisiana a few weeks later. First we met with Má and explained that we wanted to get married. "You have to get her family's permissions first," she said.

"We know," I said.

Together Lisa and I walked to her family's apartment. Taking deep breaths we knocked on the door. Lisa's brother and sister from Vietnam opened the door, and Lisa cried out and hugged them. After Lisa had a chance to talk to her siblings, we went to the living room where we saw Lisa's father. Bowing down in traditional Vietnamese fashion, we asked for his forgiveness, and I explained that I intended to convert.

Lisa's father shrugged. "What is done is already done," he said. "But now that you are converting, I think it's time to plan the wedding."

I told Má that I intended to convert, and she did not look pleased. However she understood how Lisa had sacrificed everything for me and this was something I needed to do. Chủ Bảy wasn't as understanding, but he came around. When I told Chủ Sâu, he said if I went through with it that he would disown me. No nephew of his, no man, should ever cater to a woman. I tried to reason with him, but he refused.

A couple months later, on August 10, 1991, I stood at the back of the church, waiting for someone to tell me it was time to walk down the aisle. In Vietnamese tradition, Lisa and I would walk down together to meet the priest at the altar.

Like most Vietnamese weddings, we had to invite everyone we knew, sending out over 1,000 invitations. Our wedding was going to be huge. I didn't have much time to worry about it though, the next months flew by in a rush of wedding planning and Catholic catechism classes.

A couple days before the wedding, I convinced Chú Bảy to come with me to where Chú Sáu was working in Houston. I needed to give it one more try. Maybe Chú Bảy could convince Chú Sáu to come back with us. After we drove through the night, I sat down with Chú Sáu.

"Uncle, I have come to take you back for the wedding. You're family and I really want you there," I said.

But he wouldn't come to the wedding, creating excuses and flat out refusing. I hated knowing that my uncle strongly disapproved of my marriage, but I now had a better understanding of what Lisa had been through to run away to Minnesota with me. Though she had eventually regained her family's approval, she had left Houma, assuming that she would never talk to them again. I wouldn't stop our wedding because of one man's disapproval.

I couldn't convince Chú Sáu to come back with Chú Bảy and me, and time ran out. Chú Bảy and I had to make it back for the ceremony. I could never repair my relationship with Chú Sáu, and we haven't spoken in years.

Now I was standing at the back of the church, looking at my bride as we prepared to walk down the aisle together. She beamed at me as the music began to play and we turned to look at a sea of faces. This was it. After everything we had been through, I was seeing Lisa get the wedding of her dreams. We walked down the aisle, side by side, making one final journey before our life together began.

At the altar, I looked into Lisa's face, understanding why my parents had sacrificed everything to give my siblings and I a chance for a good life. For me this was my life with Lisa. Not a day goes by when I don't think about Vietnam, where we came from, and what my family had to survive for me to be where I am today.

Dad Ed Fedler, Mom Cua Fedler, Tuần, Lisa, Lisa's mom Gioi Nguyen and dad Quyen Nguyen

Lisa and Tuần's Wedding Day

EPILOGUE

1998

THE PLANE LANDED AND TAXIED up to the gate. Over the loud-speaker, I heard familiar sounds, someone speaking my native language: "Welcome to Ho Chi Minh City."

For the first time since our terrifying escape out to sea, I was back in Vietnam.

In 1994, the United States lifted the trade embargo, and Vietnam opened its borders. Hundreds, if not thousands, of refugees flew back to visit families they hadn't seen in over a decade. Má was not an exception. She jumped at the chance to visit her mother and brothers in Vietnam.

I looked over at my kids in the seats between Lisa and me. Kenny, six, looked excited as he strained to look out the window. Kayle, who was only four, slept leaning on Lisa's shoulder. I had wanted my kids to know where they came from, but I never thought that they would have a chance to see it. The markets, the houses, the people—they would have a chance to see it all.

In the city, I saw uniformed Vietcong, and my heart sank. Did they know I had escaped? If I was put in prison, the United States wouldn't have time to get me out before something terrible happened. For the first time since I had immigrated to the United States, I felt the fear that at any moment, the Vietcong could come and take away everything that I loved.

But I wasn't the only "American Vietnamese" returning to Vietnam, so the Vietcong took no notice of my family and me. Though we all spoke Vietnamese as our first language, the country had changed, and its language changed with it. Our clothes and mannerisms were totally different from those who had stayed in Vietnam. People could tell we weren't from Vietnam anymore.

From Ho Chi Minh, we traveled south to where Bà Ngoại still lived. As we traveled through the country, everything my family had experienced—fear, hunger, violence—hit me in a wave.

Meeting my family after years of separation felt incredibly surreal, like I was traveling into the past. They all looked older and wore the hardship of their lives on their faces. Má loved being back the most, seeing her family and catching up on their lives. Unlike Ba, who had escaped with his two brothers, Má had no one from her family escape.

After my father died, Má had married Mr. Ed, an American man, who had known my father. My sister Amy was born in 1992. Sadly, Mr. Ed had died of lung cancer in 2000. Of course I experienced mixed feelings when Má remarried, but I grew to love my step-siblings—Florence and Mitchell Motes, Tina and Reece Havard, Walter and Amiee Fedler—and my stepfather. Mr. Ed looked after my mother and seemed to really care about her. I was happy if she was happy.

Now in Vietnam, I watched Má talk with her family. This seemed to be just what she needed. She was still the toughest woman I knew.

Walking around the small town, I saw a little boy standing on a corner, holding his stomach and begging for food. I knew that look, and my heart broke. Walking over, I smiled at the boy and said, "Come with me to the restaurant."

I could tell he knew I was from America and looked pleased as he followed me into the restaurant. The restaurant owner scowled down at the boy, but I ignored the man. "Bring this kid whatever he wants and I will pay for it," I said.

Still scowling, the restaurant owner nodded, and the boy and I sat down. "Order whatever you want, whatever you have been craving. You can order extra to take with you even. I don't care what it costs. I'll pay for it," I said.

The boy took me at my word, ordering huge plates of food. When the first plate was set in front of him, the boy devoured everything. It seemed as if I just turned my head for one second and the food was gone. He looked to be a little older than Kenny, and I couldn't help but think of my little brothers when we were starving and searching for snails in the mud. I may not be able to feed this boy for the rest of his life, but at least I made this day better for him. Maybe I had given him hope to keep going, to keep fighting for life.

I saw Bà Nội and Chú Út, my father's brother who had sacrificed his freedom to get us out of Vietnam. Chú Út's arm had been so badly damaged by the Vietcong that it hung limply at his side. His face looked haunted, troubled by a life of fighting for survival. His wife had never forgiven him for sacrificing everything for us. But I understood and couldn't blame her for being angry. After Kenny and Kayle were born, I understood what Chú Út had given up for us—not just his own well-being, but his children's as well.

Each day brought a new, difficult memory for me to face. I kept listening for helicopters or gunfire, but none came. On the first day in the village, a girl came up to me and offered me a lottery ticket. She looked half-starved and dirty. Of course I bought almost all of them, smiling at her.

The girl came every day after that, thinking that Americans must have all the money in the world. Near the end of our trip I asked her, "How old are you?"

"Nine," she said.

I felt the emotion rising in my chest as I thought, *That's the age I was when I had to take care of all of my siblings.* She could have been me twenty years ago.

Half-teasing, I said, "If I made you my daughter-in-law, would you come back with me to America?"

"Oh, no," she said.

I was shocked. "Why do you say that?" I asked. "Most people would jump at the chance to go to America. Why don't you want to go?"

"If I went," she said, "then who would take care of my brother and sister? And my parents?"

Tears came to my eyes. This girl, this little nine-year-old girl, had no thought for herself. She just wanted to take care of her family. How old she was for her age, especially when I thought of the prosperity and comfort my own kids had in America.

This could have been Kenny, I thought. *If my parents hadn't escaped with us, this girl could have been one of my kids. I could have been one of the parents she's talking about.*

Watching the girl scamper off with my money in-hand, I looked around at the village and thought again of everything my parents had done to help us.

"Daddy!" said Kenny as he ran out of the house and into my arms.

I picked him up and swung him around.

"Who was that?" he asked.

I didn't answer right away, and Kenny and I watched the girl run off down the street. "That's just a little girl selling tickets to help her family."

"Should I do that?" he asked.

"No, Kenny. You'll never have to do that. I promise."

Even today, there are many kids in Vietnam in the same situation I was in

ADDITIONAL AUTHOR INFORMATION

After Chuck and Lisa were married, they moved back to Minnesota so Chuck could continue college. But to pay for college, Chuck had to work all the time, and his grades suffered. Chuck and Lisa decided that he would pause his education to save money so he could finish college. But the opportunity to finish his degree never came.

After leaving college, he started working more at the grocery store and eventually became a manager. In 1993, their son Kenny was born. To better provide for his family, Chuck moved back down to Louisiana to start shrimping again. He and Lisa managed to save some money and decided to start a restaurant back up in Minnesota. In 1995, on Christmas Day, their daughter Kayle was born.

A year later, they had to close the restaurant, file for bankruptcy, and move back to Louisiana. Lisa's family started working in the nail salon business, and Lisa became a certified nail technician. At the time, Chuck was working as a paint blaster and later went on to become a welder. But in 1998 the work dried up, and Chuck thought he would give nails a try.

In 1998, Chuck and Lisa moved to Georgia to work in a nail salon belonging to Lisa's uncle. In 2001, they moved to Charleston, South Carolina, but the salon where they worked didn't have enough business for them both to work full time. Friends they worked with asked Chuck and Lisa if they wanted to buy a nail salon in nearby Greenville, South Carolina. After visiting the area, Lisa and Chuck bought the nail salon called "J Nails" in Greenville and have lived there ever since.

ENDNOTES

1. Lewy, Guenter. *America in Vietnam.* New York: Oxford University Press, 1978.

2. Herrera, Carlos E, and Surasan Sataviriya. *Water and Sanitation in Asia and the Pacific.* Singapore: WEDC Conference, 1984.

3. Lewy, Guenter. *America in Vietnam.* New York: Oxford University Press, 1978.

4. *Statistical Information about Fatal Casualties of the Vietnam War,* accessed August 2015, http://www.archives.gov/research/military/vietnam-war/casualty-statistics.html#category.

For more information about

Sand in Their Eyes
&
Chuck Doan

please visit:

www.facebook.com/charlie.doan.75

For more information about
AE BOOKS
please visit:

www.ambassador-international.com
@AmbassadorIntl
www.facebook.com/AmbassadorIntl